REflections

Book 1

Religion, people & issues

Acknowledgements

Folens Publishers would like to thank the following for giving permission to use copyright material.

Scriptures are taken from the *Good News Bible* published by The Bible Societies/Collins © American Bible Society.

Corrine Bailey Rae quote (page 45) By kind permission of NI Syndication.

Archbishop's camping holiday article (pages 52–53) By kind permission of NI Syndication.

Jo Berry and Patrick Magee article (pages 76–77) By kind permission of The Forgiveness Project www.theforgivenessproject.com.

Photographs

Actionplus: 43, 56 (right), 106 (referee)
Akg-images/ Nimatallah: 40
Alamy/ Devinder Sangha: 123
Alamy/ Fredrik Renander: 84/85 (background)
Alamy/ Greenshoots Communications: 61
Alamy/ Indiapicture: 98 (bottom)
Alamy/ Janine Wiedel Photo Library: 48, 117
Alamy/ Kolvenbach: 86
Alamy/ Mike Abrahams: 77
Alamy/ Nordic Photos: 113 (middle)
Alamy/ Simon Belcher: 23 (bottom)
Alamy/ World Religions Photo Library: 46, 106 (court of law)
Andes Press Agency/ Carlos Reyes Manzo: 113 (bottom right)
Ardea.com/ Jean Michel Labat: 14 (bottom)
Art Directors & Trip Photo Library: 47, 114
Art Directors & Trip Photo Library/ Helene Rogers: 50, 57 (top), 92 (bottom), 104/105 (Torah scrolls), 109
Bhaktivedanta Book Trust International Inc © 2007: 39
Circa Photo Library/ John Smith: 113 (top right), 119
Corbis/ Ali Haider/ EPA: 96
Corbis/ Blaine Harrington III: 99 (top)
Corbis/ David Turnley: 70
Corbis/ ESA/ Hubble Collaboration/ Handout/ CNP: 13 (background)
Corbis / image 100: 74
Corbis/ Michael St Maur Sheil: 84 (cenotaph), 102
Corbis/ National Museum of Ethiopia/ EPA: 13
Corbis/ Nik Wheeler: 5, 6
Corbis/ Pascal Deloche/ Godong: 57 (bottom)
Corbis/ Paul Hardy: 22 (bottom)
Corbis/ Reuters: 72, 85 (mosque)
Corbis/ Reuters/ Natalie Behring Chisholm: 32/33
Corbis/ Salvatore di Nolfi/ EPA: 17 (bottom)
Empics/ ABACA Press: 79 (bottom)
Empics/ AP: 9, 54, 59, 79 (top), 108
Empics/ PA: 78 (bottom right), 87
Farmington Trust/ Stephen Bird: 36–37
www.theforgivenessproject.com: 76
Getty/ Abid Katib: 97
Getty/ Hulton Archive: 74
Getty/ Jacob Silberberg: 42, 49 (top)
Hatton Operatic Society: 25
Judi and Ian Hunter: 106 (wedding), 121
istockphoto: 17 (top), 23 (top), 105 (Bible)
istockphoto/ Kenneth C Zirkel: 20
istockphoto/ Nancy Louie: 89
istockphoto/ Nicholas Roemmelt: 16
istockphoto/ Ron Hohenhaus: 118
istockphoto/ Sorem Pilman: 103
istockphoto/ Steven Allan: 104/105 (Qur'an), 115
John Birdsall Photography www.johnbirdsall.co.uk: 91

Martin Sheppard/ Diocese of York: 53
NASA: 14 (top)
2007 Nokia: 44
Offside Sports Photography: 92 (top)
Photos.com/ Jupiterimages: 49 (left)
Photofusion: 106 (policewoman)
Reportdigital/ Justin Tallis: 63 (top)
Reportdigital/ Stefano Cagnoli: 34
Rex Features Ltd: 11
Rex Features Ltd: 62
Rex Features Ltd/ ABC/ Medya Ajansi: 56 (left)
Rex Features Ltd/ Alban pix Ltd: 66
Rex Features Ltd/ Alix/ Phanie: 63 (middle left)
Rex Features Ltd/ Andrea Boohers: 8, 19
Rex Features/ Jon Beretta: 68
Rex Features Ltd/ David Fisher: 45
Rex Features Ltd/ IPC Magazines/ Chat: 113 (left)
Rex Features Ltd/ Jonathan Player: 78 (left)
Rex Features Ltd/ Fotex: 63 (bottom)
Rex Features Ltd/ Frank Monaco: 51
Rex Features Ltd/ Kippa Matthews: 52
Rex Features Ltd/ Sipa Press: 83
Ronald Grant Archive/ Universal Pictures: 30 (top), 69, 78/79
Ina Taylor: 15, 30 (bottom), 94, 95, 98 (top), 99 (bottom), 101, 119
Topfoto/ UPPA: 71, 81

© 2007 Folens Limited, on behalf of the author.

United Kingdom: Folens Publishers, Apex Business Centre, Boscombe Road, Dunstable, LU5 4RL
Email: folens@folens.com

Ireland: Folens Publishers, Greenhills Road, Tallaght, Dublin 24.
Email: info@folens.ie

Poland: JUKA, ul. Renesansowa 38, Warsaw 01-905

Editor: Judi Hunter, Spellbound Books
Text design and layout: eMC Design Ltd, www.emcdesign.org.uk
Picture researcher: Sue Sharp
Illustrations: JB Illustrations
Cover design: Neil Hawkins, ndesign.co.uk
Cover image: iStock

First published 2007 by Folens Limited.

Every effort has been made to contact copyright holders of material used in this publication. If any copyright holder has been overlooked, we should be pleased to make any necessary arrangements.

British Library Cataloguing in Publication Data. A catalogue record for this publication is available from the British Library.

ISBN   978-1-85008-212-5

Contents

Looking for answers to difficult questions

Every so often you probably stop and wonder what the point of everything is. What are we supposed to be doing here, on this planet, at this time? Perhaps there isn't any point at all.

In this unit we will look at how some people find meaning in their lives, and the answers religion offers.

1.1 Try to decide whether it is ever possible to understand life.

1.2 Consider whether or not humans are simply animals.

1.3 Look at different responses to the idea that God knows the answers.

1.4 Examine what Christians think about life and humanity.

1.5 Examine the way people who do not believe in God make sense of life.

What's going on?

Can you see the big picture?

Sometimes it is difficult to understand what is going on when you are right in the middle of it. Only when you stand back can you see the whole picture. Could this be true of life? Not everyone agrees that there is any picture there anyway. What do you think?

> Oh no you can't!

If the person on the left in this picture was brought to this place blindfolded and then allowed to look at his surroundings, he would never guess where he was. His view would be like the one on page 5. Here, we can see where he actually is. He is standing in the middle of a white horse carved in ancient times into the chalk downs of Wiltshire. Some might say this shows just how impossible it is for us to understand what we are doing in this life. We are too close to it at the moment. Just because we can't understand the purpose of our life, doesn't mean there isn't one.

> 'The reason you can't see any point in life is because there isn't one! It's chance the way things have worked out. I'd say it is all a mess and I'm in the middle of it.'

It only makes sense when you can stand back and look.

> It is all a mess anyway!

Some people think that the reason we find it difficult to make sense of what we are doing on the planet is because there isn't any point to it. Things have just happened and there is no logical order to them. If you throw a few pebbles down on the ground, there is no particular order to the way they fall. But sit and study them long enough and you can probably invent some sort of pattern.

> *Oh yes you can!*

You might have expected religion and science to be on opposite sides. Below, they are agreeing with each other.

Let's consider the scientific view

Scientists do not think everything is a random mess. Quite the opposite! They are sure that life on the earth, and in outer space, obeys very strict rules. It is the job of science to discover and understand what rules the universe obeys.

The scientist Charles Darwin did not think human life was a mess or just the result of an accident. He saw clear evidence of animals evolving and adapting to their environment.

Let's consider the religious view

Those people who belong to a religion – remember scientists can have religious views just like everyone else – say there is a clear purpose to life. Nothing is random or chaotic. Everything has been created for a reason and we are part of a bigger picture. In fact, we have a very important part to play in that picture. Followers of all the different world religions believe we have been created by a higher being.

> '*I don't believe something so wonderful as this life, on this planet, would happen just by accident. There has to be something behind it all. I am sure there is something good behind it all. You can call it God if you want to. The name doesn't matter to me.*'

To finish

There are four arguments on these pages. Two explain why we can't understand what we are doing in this life. Two say we can understand.

a Divide your page into four boxes.

b Write each of the arguments in a box.

c Outline in colour the box which is closest to your ideas.

Smart animals?

Some people say that we are no more than the smartest animals in the pack. Others say humans are quite different. Let's examine the evidence.

The dog in this picture is searching the rubble for survivors. He is far better at this job than any human. Does that make him superior?

 Us and them

Man evolving from an ape (see page 7) shows one idea of where we stand in the animal kingdom. Some say we have simply evolved to become the best animal – that's all. Others say there is such a big difference between us and animals, we are more distinctly different.

1 *Divide your page into two columns.*

   a In the left-hand column, list all the things a dog can do that a human can't.

   b In the right-hand column, list all the things a human can do that a dog can't.

   c Underneath, write whether you think we are better than animals or simply different. Give a reason.

 Don't ask questions

One thing that makes us different from animals is that we question. The dog in the picture is likely to have been brought to the scene by his handler and set to work. Unless he is a difficult dog who wants to play or run off, he would have gone straight in and begun the search. By contrast, his handler would find out as much as possible about the task by asking questions before he starts work.

Koko, the gorilla, has lived with scientist Dr Penny Patterson for 30 years and has been brought up like a human child. Penny has taught Koko sign language. The gorilla can sign 1000 words and hold simple conversations.

Fruit
Nose
Hungry
Tickle
Good
Time
Gorilla
Tiger
Eat
Love
Drink
Mother

We can't be sure that animals don't question things. They can't speak so we don't know what is going on in their minds. Many pet owners would say their pets do ask questions. A certain look or behaviour seems to be asking 'Is it dinner time?' or 'Am I going out?' It is unlikely an animal asks *why* something is happening. Asking why and working out reasons appears to be something humans do and animals don't. Does this make us superior?

We share 99% of the same DNA as chimpanzees, so are we simply smart monkeys?

2 *Use the Internet to discover more about Dr Penny Patterson's interesting experiment. What question would you most like to ask Koko?*

> How do we differ from animals?

Humans are unique because they are capable of emotions like love, laughter and humour. Humans also have a sense of the past, present and future. We plan for the future and learn from the past. This enables us to pass knowledge on to our children, so they are better informed from the outset. We seem to progress in intelligence in a way animals don't.

> What do Christians say?

Christians don't think humans are just smart animals. The Bible says God created the world, plant life and then animals. It goes on to say, finally, God created humans. So Christians understand humans are distinct from animals. Because we have higher intellectual and emotional powers, Christians believe we are capable of a personal relationship with our creator, God. Now that does put us in a different category to animals.

To finish

3 *Design a poster with an outline of a human in the centre. Surround the person with arguments to show that either:*
   ● *humans are just smart animals*
   or:
   ● *humans are more than smart animals.*

It is natural to search for answers. It is one of the things that make us human. Here, we examine some different responses to the idea that God has the answers.

I don't believe God exists. Call me an **atheist**. I don't think there are any 'magic' answers out there. There is no big daddy figure behind things. You have got to work it out for yourself.

Just because you can't see the answer easily, doesn't mean there isn't one. Remember that person standing next to the White Horse on page 5? We are never going to understand things from where we are standing. Do I believe in God? Don't know really. Call me an **agnostic** because I am not sure. I suppose it is possible there is a God but because we are only human we are never going to be clever enough to be certain.

1 Draw the outline of a head with a speech bubble. Inside the speech bubble write your thoughts on whether God is the answer.

It is worth deciding first whether you believe there is any pattern to life, or whether you think life is completely haphazard. If there is a pattern, did it happen by chance or by design?

Everything that happens is part of something bigger. Yes, of course it is hard to see what is going on sometimes. I often feel like a piece of this jigsaw puzzle, but one without the box that's got the picture on! Just because we can't see the whole picture, doesn't mean there isn't one.

I am sure there is a force more powerful than us who created the world we are in. I call that force God. Everything is too well organised and intricate to be the result of chance. I am a **theist**, I believe in God.

> ## There is something smart behind this!

An increasing number of people are convinced that human life did not happen by accident. They believe something so brilliant must have a reason. For them, the evidence points to an intelligent force that designed things to be the way they are. If you look at a human brain, or even an eye, it is an incredibly complicated mechanism that does its job superbly. It is hard to know how to improve it. It is evidence like this that convinces people there must be a God.

2 *What do you think the atheist would say was the reason for the complexity of the human eye? Would you agree?*

To finish

3 *Can you write some brief notes for the radio presenter Chris Filton? He is going to interview Charlene (an **atheist**), Ben (an **agnostic**) and Paul (a **theist**) on his Thursday show. They are going to be talking about serious issues, such as why there is evil in the world and why innocent people get hurt. Chris needs to know something about his guests before he plans his questions.*

Christians find answers

Christians believe God is the key to life. Here, we examine what they mean.

> An intelligent designer

Christians are sure there is something intelligent behind the universe. It is too intricate to happen by accident, it must have been designed. They call this designer God and believe God is both a powerful and good force. Out of love God created the universe, the earth and all forms of life. These are mind-blowing concepts that are hard to get your head around.

> Creation according to the Bible

Day 1: God created the earth and the sea out of nothing.

Day 2: God made the sky above the earth and created day and night.

Day 3: God created plant life.

Day 4: God created the sun, moon and stars.

Day 5: God created birds and sea life.

Day 6: God created animals and then God created humans.

Day 7: Because His creation was finished, God rested.

Is this just a cartoon story?

Christians disagree about how literally this creation story should be taken. Some say it was just a fable to help ancient people understand how the world began. Others say that it is exactly how it happened – and in seven days.

Almost everyone, Christians and atheists alike, agree that the order in which things happened is probably correct. First, the planet was formed, then plant life appeared, then sea and bird life and, finally, animal life. Humans came on the scene a bit later. For Christians, God is the key to understanding why things happened as they did.

1 *Find out what the Big Bang Theory is and write three sentences to explain it. Do you think it is possible for a Christian to believe in this theory and accept the creation story on the left? Why?*

Where do people fit into this?

The creation story does include people and says animals were created before humans. The Bible story goes on to say:

'God created human beings making them to be like himself' (Genesis 1:27).

These words, and the idea that God made humans after he made animals, have convinced Christians we are special. They don't accept the idea that we are just smart animals. For them, humans are distinctly different and deliberately created by God. For these reasons, we are capable of having a personal relationship with God. Many Christians find it helpful to think of God as a father-figure who made us and cares for us.

Men from monkeys?

On page 7 we saw pictures of the evolution of humans from apes. This is based on Darwin's Theory of Evolution. Some Christians do not agree with this theory. They believe people were created as a distinct species by an intelligent designer and never evolved from monkeys. They would not accept this skull as an early person but more likely the baby of a breed of monkey that died out.

Other Christians have no difficulty in accepting both Darwin's theory and the biblical creation story. This is because they believe evolution was part of God's plan to create humans. The skull shown here could be evidence of that.

To finish

2 *Write the words 'Intelligent Designer' in the centre of your page. Create a mind map around the word 'Intelligent' using one colour. Then do the same around the word 'Designer' using a different colour.*

This skull was discovered in Ethiopia early in the twenty-first century. It is thought to belong to a youngster who lived 3.3 million years ago. Early reconstruction suggests she looked partly ape and partly human.

Here, we consider whether it is possible to make sense of life and enjoy it if you don't believe in God.

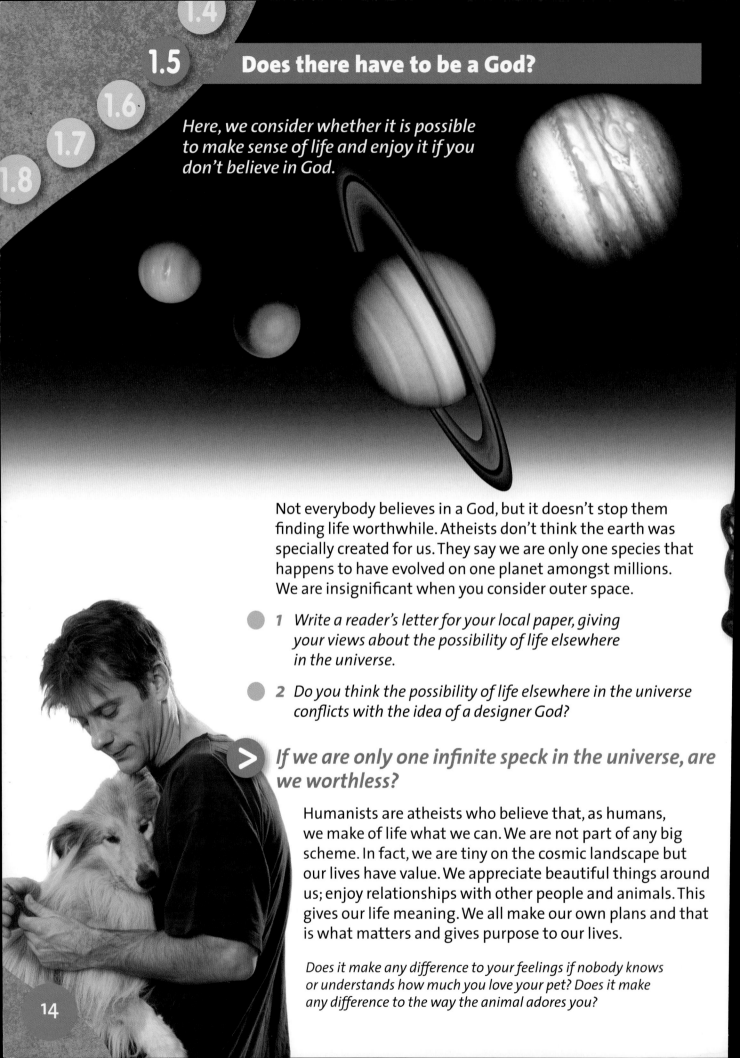

Not everybody believes in a God, but it doesn't stop them finding life worthwhile. Atheists don't think the earth was specially created for us. They say we are only one species that happens to have evolved on one planet amongst millions. We are insignificant when you consider outer space.

1 *Write a reader's letter for your local paper, giving your views about the possibility of life elsewhere in the universe.*

2 *Do you think the possibility of life elsewhere in the universe conflicts with the idea of a designer God?*

> *If we are only one infinite speck in the universe, are we worthless?*

Humanists are atheists who believe that, as humans, we make of life what we can. We are not part of any big scheme. In fact, we are tiny on the cosmic landscape but our lives have value. We appreciate beautiful things around us; enjoy relationships with other people and animals. This gives our life meaning. We all make our own plans and that is what matters and gives purpose to our lives.

Does it make any difference to your feelings if nobody knows or understands how much you love your pet? Does it make any difference to the way the animal adores you?

Buddhism is a world religion that does not believe there is a God. The Buddha was an ordinary person who faced normal problems, such as being ill, getting old and dying, even though he was born into a wealthy family. In an effort to understand why suffering like this happened to people, the Buddha went off alone to think. He did not turn to any God or higher power for the answer. He thought it out for himself.

> *What do you really, really want?*

3 *Think of three things you want right now. (This is a personal exercise, so don't feel obliged to share your ideas with anyone else.) Choose one thing and decide why you really want it.*

The chances are that, when you have thought it through, you will come to the conclusion that the basic reason why you want what you do is because it will make you happy. When you are happy, you will be perfectly content. End of story!

The Buddha decided that basically what everyone wants from life is contentment. Things that get in the way of our contentment make us unhappy. The way to enjoy life is to be content.

> *So have Buddhists made sense of life?*

Yes, they believe they have. Like the Humanists, Buddhists don't look for any God to solve things. They say that the answer to happiness in life lies within ourselves.

To finish

4 *Copy these two sentences below, choosing the ending you think works best.*

    a The Buddha decided people would be happy and content if...
- *...they had lots of money*
- *...they believed in God*
- *...they were satisfied with what they had.*

    b Humanists think we can be happy in life without a God if...
- *...we make lots of plans*
- *...we have good relationships with other people*
- *...we make the best of what we've got.*

5 *Where do people like Buddhists and Humanists look for answers? Do you think they are right? Why?*

1 *What is each picture saying about someone's view of life?*

2 *What image would you choose to reflect your idea of life? (It doesn't have to be one of these.)*

ARATHON 2006

All through this unit of work we have been asking 'What's going on?' We thought about the sort of questions people ask and looked at the way people try to find answers.

Write down three questions that this unit has made you think about.

 Let's remind ourselves of what we have learned:

We began by wondering whether it is possible for humans to ever know enough to come up with answers. **A** Why do some people say, 'You'll never understand what's going on in life'? **B** What would scientists say to the idea that life is a random mess?	**We considered** the different ideas people have about the beginning of the world, and went on to examine whether people are any different from others in the animal kingdom. **A** Give one idea about how the world began. **B** How different do you think humans are from animals?
We looked in detail at Christian ideas about creation and the importance of humans. **A** What do Christians mean by a 'designer God'? **B** Do Christians think humans are the same as animals?	**We went on to examine** how people of no religious belief or Buddhists (who do not believe in God) find answers to these difficult questions. **A** How do Buddhists make sense of life? **B** What do Humanists say makes life worthwhile?

What sort of questions does this picture raise about animal intelligence?

Choose one of these tasks to check your progress in this unit.

Task one

a Give two reasons why an atheist (someone who does not believe in God) would say the world just happened.

b Give two reasons why a Christian would disagree.

c How do you think something as intricate as the human brain might have come about? Explain your reasons.

Task two

a Why do some people say humans are just smart animals?

b Most Christians would not agree that humans are just smart animals. Why?

c Give three examples of things that make human beings special. Then give your thoughts on how this has happened.

1.8   Something extra

This model gives an idea of the complexity of the human brain. Although scientists and doctors have come a long way in understanding how the brain works, they admit there is a huge amount they don't know. They can't see an idea in the brain.

1 *a* How would a religious person use this model above as proof of the existence of God?

   b Why wouldn't this convince a Humanist of the existence of God?

2 Write each of the following six statements on a slip of paper. Drop them into a box. Six people then select one each and explain what it means.

Humans are just smart animals – no more, no less.

Humans are unique.

The world is too complex to have happened by chance.

God created humans in his own image.

The only way to enjoy life is to be content with what you have got.

It's not God who gives meaning to our life, it's the relationships we make.

3 Cut out three head and shoulders pictures from a magazine and stick them on a large sheet of paper. Give each person a speech bubble.

   a One person is an agnostic. What will they say about their belief in God and the creation of the world?

   b The second person is a theist. What will they say about their belief in God and the creation of the world?

   c The third person is an atheist. What will they say about their belief in God and the creation of the world?

4 *a* Research four facts about the Milky Way and write them in your book.

   b Which is the most mind-blowing of these facts?

   c Would any of these facts convince you of the existence of God? Why?

5 The Buddha was the founder of one of the six great world religions – Buddhism. This is a religion which does not believe in the existence of God.

   Find out what happened in the Buddha's life that led him to believe that the meaning of life was within ourselves.

6 The skull nicknamed 'Lucy's baby' appeared on page 13 as a recent archaeological find that challenges theories of evolution.

   a Find out about another twenty-first-century discovery nicknamed 'The Hobbit'. This skeleton is also called by its technical name *homo floresiensis.* You could use the Internet to help with your research.

   b What did people claim about this skeleton at the time?

   c What is the current thinking?

   d What has any of this got to do with RE?

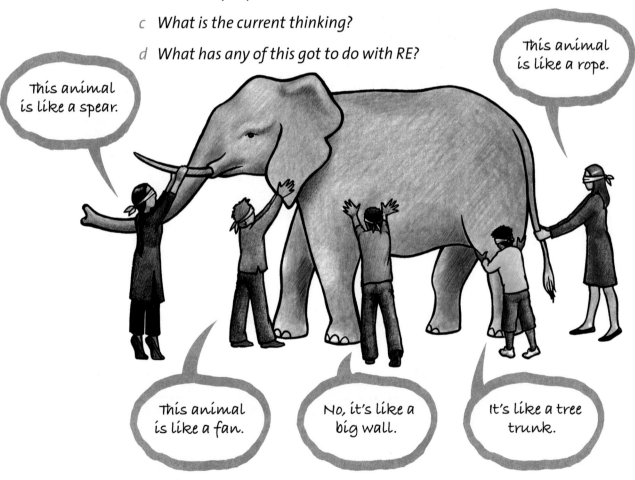

7 *a* What is the connection between this cartoon and the picture that opened this unit on page 5?

   b What has this cartoon got to do with people's ideas about God?

Life after death

In this unit we ask the big question, 'What happens after we die?' Then we examine a variety of beliefs, including those held by people who do not believe in a God but still think there is life after death.

2.1 Consider the variety of ideas people hold about what happens after we die.

2.2 Look at the supernatural experiences and beliefs of people who do not believe in a God.

2.3 Study Christian beliefs and the reasons for them.

2.4 Examine a key piece of Christian evidence in detail.

2.5 Consider religious belief that involves reincarnation.

2.6 Examine whether or not what you do really matters.

Whatever next?

Here, we look at some ideas people have about what happens after we die.

What is the difference? Which is your idea of life after death?

> ## Do people believe in life after death?

The surprise result of a recent British survey was that 70% of people questioned believed in some sort of life after death. Interestingly, most said they didn't belong to a religion. When asked what they thought life after death would be like, their ideas differed widely and many simply weren't sure. They just knew death wasn't the end.

Followers of the major world religions all agree there is some existence after death that goes on forever. Christians, Jews and Muslims believe we have one earthly life and another spiritual life with God. The Eastern religions, Buddhism, Sikhism and Hinduism, teach that we live many lives on earth until we reach the right stage to move on to a spiritual existence.

 1 *a Conduct your own survey as a class. Decide the best way to phrase a question to ask people if they believe in any form of existence after death. Don't make it especially religious because ghosts need to be permitted. If everybody asks five people of different ages, you will get a useful sample.*

   b Collect the results. Plot your data as a graph or on a spreadsheet and compare the outcome with the national survey.

> ## Let's look at the idea of death as a full stop

 30% of those surveyed said that when you die that's it. Nothing. Oblivion. This might seem very depressing but the Humanists, who do not believe in any God, disagree. They say that because this is the only life we have, it is really special. For them, the only afterlife is in people's memories or through our children, or as a result of things we did in our lifetime.

> Could life after death be green?

It is a scientific fact that you can **never destroy energy**, you can **only change its form**. This means that when the body of any living being dies, it turns into something else. In the ground it becomes compost to provide life for new plants. Plants are part of the food chain, and so it goes on. There is no difference if the body is cremated because ash also provides nutrients for plants. Would you call this everlasting life?

At a dress rehearsal people make mistakes, forget their lines and take too long changing but it is good practice for the real performance. What do people mean when they say, 'Life is not a dress rehearsal'?

> Been there, done that

Have you ever had the feeling that you have been somewhere before, yet you couldn't possibly have been. This is known as déjà vu. For some people, this feeling convinces them that they have lived on earth before. Living another life on earth is called reincarnation.

To finish

2 a *Draw a diagram to show three different views about life after death.*
  - *One view is that death is the end.*
  - *A second view is that there is life after death.*
  - *A third view is that we live many lives on earth.*
 b *Which comes closest to your own view? Write a sentence saying why you agree with this view.*

Is it just for the religious?

Let's examine what people who are not religious think about life after death.

> No, I'm not religious, but I do think there is something after you die. How do you explain near-death experiences?

> What are near-death experiences?

These are cases where people go through some sort of trauma and are clinically dead. Often this happens on the operating table when the patient's heart stops but they are eventually revived. What is interesting about these cases is that some people have memories of being dead for that short time. They all describe the same thing. They saw a long tunnel with a bright light at the end and felt drawn along the tunnel. Before they reached the end of the tunnel they were revived. All said they had not wanted to return to life because everything was so beautiful and peaceful at the end of the tunnel.

The near-death experience changed these people's lives. They were no longer scared of dying because they felt sure they had glimpsed a life after death – heaven, if you want to call it that – and it was wonderful.

 1 *If one of these people who had a near-death experience was on a radio phone-in, which two questions would you like to ask them?*

> What do scientists think about life after death?

Some scientists certainly do think everything stops with death. Others point to the fact that the body and mind can live separately. A person can be 'brain dead' even though their body is functioning on a life-support machine. So, if the body can live on without the brain, could the brain carry on after the body is dead?

There is also the idea of a 'green' life after death that we considered on page 25. Scientifically, nothing can be destroyed, but only changed into another form.

Science certainly doesn't rule out life after death. There are plenty of things we can't see but we know exist. The best brain surgeon in the world can't look inside a person's head and find an idea. But we know the idea exists.

Do you believe in me?

> **Let's consider close encounters of the spooky kind**

Ghosts are very popular. Lots of people believe in them even if they haven't seen one. A ghost is the spirit of a dead person that can be seen by the living. Ghosts are alleged to do all sorts of things from quietly wandering around to nosily throwing objects about. Occasionally, there are accounts of ghosts bringing warnings to people, but usually ghosts go on their way unaware of the living.

● **2** *Ghosts: True or False?*
  What do you think?

● **3** *Work out what the similarity is between death and birth. Does this argument on the right convince you that there might be something out there? Why?*

I don't think we can ever know about anything like this. Death is like birth. We emerge into a world we don't know.

> **Perhaps the whole thing is impossible to get to grips with**

This person is saying death is like birth. That is an unusual slant! Most of us would never think they are similar.

To finish

● **4** *Choose one of the four points made here that interests you. Display the idea as a poster to help a person to understand it.*

2.3   Christian belief

Here, we examine what Christians believe happens after we die.

 What do Christians believe?

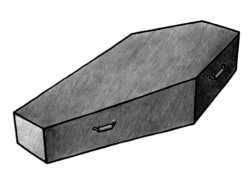

Birth – Most Christians are convinced we only have one life that begins when we are born.

Living – Whilst on earth, we have to try and lead a good life.

Death – At some point everyone will die, their body will stop.

Judgement – After a person's death, God will judge them. God will look at everything that person did, said and thought in their lifetime. Those judged good will be rewarded; those who have been evil will be punished.

Everlasting life – Although the body stops, the soul carries on forever.

 How do you get your head around this?

It is difficult to imagine what death might be like because we are only at the start of our lives. Some people think the lifecycle of a butterfly is a helpful image. First, there is the caterpillar; this then turns into a chrysalis. Then it rests for a while; eventually the chrysalis opens into a beautiful butterfly. It is hard to imagine that the butterfly has any memory of being a caterpillar or a chrysalis.

The caterpillar and butterfly are totally different creatures but something must be continuing from one stage to another. What is the connection with the Christian idea in the timeline on page 28?

1 *Sketch the three stages of the butterfly's lifecycle. Against each, write which stage is supposed to be life, death and everlasting life.*

What makes Christians certain there is life after death?

The simple answer is Jesus. He helped his followers to understand the concept through his teachings and his own actions.

Let's look at what Jesus said:

> 'Do not be worried and upset,' Jesus told them. 'Believe in God and believe also in me. There are many rooms in my Father's house, and I am going to prepare a place for you. I would not tell you this if it were not so. And after I go and prepare a place for you, I will come back and take you to myself, so that you will be where I am.' (John 14:1–3)

2 *Explain what this Bible passage has to do with life after death.*

Actions speak louder than words

What usually convinces people more than words, are actions. There are several accounts of Jesus bringing people back to life but, most impressively, he came back to life himself after he had been killed. It is Jesus' own Resurrection that convinces Christians that death is not the end.

3 **a** *Look at the account of Jesus bringing a boy back to life in Luke 7:11–15.*

   b *Write a report a 'Ten O'Clock News' reporter can deliver to the camera. The reporter does not have to be a Christian; he just needs to state what happened in the town of Nain.*

To finish

4 *Write an entry for Wikipedia (the online encyclopaedia) that states what Christians believe about life after death.*

Case study of the Resurrection

Because Jesus' Resurrection is such an important piece of evidence to Christians, it needs examining in detail so you can form your own conclusions.

> What happened first?

Jesus was executed on a Friday morning. He was hoisted on to a cross of wood and held in place with nails through his hands and feet. Although he was weak from torture and bleeding wounds, he died of suffocation. This was because his body kept slumping forward. Eventually, his weight trapped his lungs and made it impossible for him to breathe.

> Was Jesus really dead?

The executioners, who were Roman soldiers, were keen to check their prisoner was dead so they could go off duty. They used the normal method. A spear was pierced into the side of Jesus' body on the cross. No blood spurted out as it would have done had Jesus been alive. Instead, only blood and watery serum oozed from the wound. This showed that the heart was no longer pumping blood around the body. Jesus was dead. So the body was taken down and left for his friends to deal with.

This rock was used to seal a cave tomb in Jerusalem in early times.

> What happened next?

Because it was late in the day, Jesus' friends wrapped his corpse up in a clean white cloth. The body was placed in a cool cave and a large rock pushed in front to keep animals out. The friends intended to return after the weekend to carry out the normal burial preparations before putting Jesus' body in a grave.

> Here is the strange bit

On the Sunday morning, some of Jesus' women followers appeared carrying materials to wash and prepare his body for the grave. When they got to the cave, they found the boulder pushed aside. Jesus' body was gone but the white cloth was still there.

> Who were the witnesses?

The Bible contains four accounts of this extraordinary event and they are all slightly different. They appear in Matthew 28:1–8; Mark 16:1–8; Luke 24:1–12; and John 20:1–10.

1 In groups of four, each person takes one Bible account listed above and notes the details. As a group, compare your accounts and spot the differences!

Mary Magdalene is the name that comes up every time as the person who got to the empty cave first.

2 Write Mary's blog about what she has seen and what she thinks has happened.

After this event, there are accounts of Jesus appearing at various times to different people. You might say that it was wishful thinking. People who loved Jesus were so upset by his death they couldn't believe it. They kept expecting he would walk in the door again and their imagination did the rest. That's possible, but how do you explain Jesus' appearance before a crowd? Is it possible for many people to imagine they had seen Jesus at the same time?

> What do you think?

3 a Read again through the information that is given on these pages. List all the evidence that shows Jesus was definitely dead.

b List the evidence given to prove Jesus came to life again.

c What do you think happened?

Remember

Christians say this story proves that there is life after death. They also believe that, by allowing himself to be executed for a crime he didn't commit, Jesus ensured people would have life after death like him.

Let's look at a different religious view of life after death.

The idea of reincarnation may seem totally natural. Think about the way a tree passes through the seasons. The branch develops buds that open to leaves, flowers and fruits. In the autumn, the leaves fall and the tree appears dead but after a few months the process begins again. The leaves that appear next year look identical but they are not the same ones.

> The treadmill

The Eastern religions, Hinduism, Sikhism and Buddhism, also see life as a journey but one that goes around in circles. They believe we have to make progress in life and, because there is too much to learn in one life, we lead many, many lives on earth. Eventually, when we have understood all there is to learn, we can escape the endless circle of life and death for a better, permanent existence elsewhere.

1 *Draw a cartoon to show the treadmill of life and death and life and death and...*

> Is it a circle or a ladder?

Whilst the Hindu idea of reincarnation involves coming back to earth as another being, it may not be as a human being. They believe everything works up the rungs of existence. This includes stones and insects, as well as humans and animals. Hindus are sure that what we do in life will affect our rebirth. So a bad person may be reborn as a lower form, like an animal. When you get to the very top rung of the ladder, you will be able to escape from earth and be united with the great eternal spirit of the universe called Brahman.

2 a *Look forward to the Hindu image of reincarnation on page 39. Write a caption for this picture.*

   b *How do you know which is death and which is birth in the picture?*

Not reincarnation but rebirth

Whilst Hindus think of one person being reborn as another person, Buddhists say it is not quite like this. They do not think there is one particular part of us that moves into the next person. They say it is just our life force that moves on. Here is a thought that will boggle your mind a bit more... Buddhists think that it is possible for parts of this life force to be reborn in more than one person at a time!

 How can you be sure?

You might think it is easy to prove whether reincarnation is true because you would remember. But the Eastern religions say that we do not carry memory from one life to another. How can you be sure? You can't! It is all down to what you believe. So what do you think?

To finish

3 What is the connection between the tree on page 32 and reincarnation?

4 Write a web page about reincarnation for a website titled 'Beliefs'.

Some people find this a useful image of rebirth. In this picture a flame has been passed along the line. But you cannot say it is exactly the same flame that is moving down the row, can you? Why?

Most people agree that what you do in your life matters, but when and how?

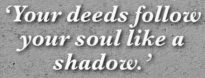

'Your deeds follow your soul like a shadow.'

What does this mean for a person?

> A cause and an effect

Although ideas vary about what happens after we die, there is great similarity about one thing. Whatever you do has consequences.

This is supported by scientific evidence too.

If someone sprays lots of pesticides on a field, the insect population dies.

No insects, means poor pollination.

Poor pollination leads to a poor crop which means less food for us.

1 *Add two more events to the chain of consequences above.*

Put simply, everything has a cause and an effect.

> Will you be punished for your bad actions?

Christians, Jews and Muslims believe God knows everything we do, say or even think. When we get to the end of our life, God will judge us on these things. There will be rewards for the good and punishments for the bad. Followers of these religions say that is perfectly sensible. What is the point of life if there is nothing at the end of it?

2 *What do you say to this?*

The idea of judgement is not new. Ancient Egyptian wall paintings show that Egyptians believed that, after death, their souls would be weighed to see how much bad and good was in them. As you might guess, bad souls weighed heavy and punishments were waiting! Look at page 40, or the whiteboard activity, to compare one of these ancient Judgement Day pictures with a modern one.

Maybe you don't get punished for your bad actions. Perhaps they punish you!

Believers in reincarnation say there is no judge out there watching everything we do, keeping an account ready to make us pay for it. We do it to ourselves. Everything has consequences. You can't escape from that. It is called karma.

These cartoons give you some idea of the immediate consequences of an action, but that is rarely the end of the story.

Who is sending out good vibes and bad vibes in these cartoons?
A Hindu would call it good and bad karma

3 *Study the cartoons above. Write or draw what might happen next in each situation.*

> *What goes around, comes around*

We can all think of a situation where somebody does something cruel and seems to get away with it. A Hindu would say that the bad karma they have created will affect them. They cannot escape it. It may not be immediately. It could even be in their next life when they are reborn lower down the scale.

4 *Write an explanation of the saying 'What goes around, comes around'. It needs to be suitable for an eight year old to understand. You might like to weave the saying into a story to show what you mean.*

Remember

Many people agree that if we do good in life, we will benefit, and if we do bad, we will suffer. Christians, Jews and Muslims believe God is the one who makes these judgements. Followers of the Eastern religions think our actions have their own built-in rewards and punishments.

Intercession of the Virgin Mary

1 *This scene is connected with the moment of death. As the man and woman climb the stairs, Mary is on the telephone. In her hand is a directory with everybody in it. Who do you think she is phoning and what will she be telling them? Where do you think the man and woman are going?*

You can read more about intercession on page 50.

The Last Judgement is a twenty-first-century painting. What modern ideas can you see in it? What do you think each picture is saying?

2 These are three deadly sins lazing around in a pub. Gluttony is shown as three figures who are feasting wearing paper crowns from Christmas crackers. Sloth, asleep on the ground, is also symbolised by the cat. Avarice, which means greed for money, sits and counts his gold. Why do you think the artist chose to set this in a pub?

3 Hell is an underground concrete car park with plenty of space for everyone. It goes on forever and it is clearly man-made. There is no time limit and no charge. What idea of hell does this give you?

37

All through this unit of work we have been asking 'Whatever next?' We have been looking at different ideas people hold about what happens to us after we die.

 Let's remind ourselves of what we have learned:

We began by looking at the two basic ideas: death is the end; and after death there is something different. **A** What do people who say death is a full stop think? **B** What do people who say death is a comma think?	**We looked in detail** at Christian beliefs based on Jesus' Resurrection. **A** What does the Resurrection of Jesus mean? **B** What difference does Jesus' Resurrection make to Christians?
We considered various ideas about life after death, including reincarnation. **A** What does reincarnation mean? **B** Why do Hindus think we need to be reincarnated?	**We went on to examine** whether our life on earth has any consequences. **A** What does karma mean? **B** What do Christians think happens on Judgement Day?

We began by considering whether death was a comma or a full stop. Which did you think it might be at the start of this study? Did any of the ideas you came across in the unit make you think again? Why?

Look at this Hindu image of reincarnation. What is happening when a person dies?
What is happening in the animal kingdom?

Choose one of these tasks to check your progress in this unit.

Task one

    a *What do Christians believe happened to Jesus after he died?*

    b *Why is this belief important to them?*

    c *Explain what you think happens after we die, and why you think this.*

Task two

    a *What do people mean by reincarnation?*

    b *Why might belief in the Day of Judgement affect a person's behaviour?*

    c *What is the difference between what a Christian believes will happen after they die and what a Hindu believes? What do you think will happen? Why?*

1   Make a mind map of the different ideas you have learned about life after death. Which idea is nearest to your own thoughts on this subject?

2   Make up your own recipe for gaining a place in heaven.

Just like any other recipe you are going to need **ingredients**. These will be the sort of personal qualities you think someone needs. It might be kindness or a sense of humour. Then, you will require the **method**. Here, you need to decide how a person will use their qualities in life. In other words, how will they treat people or the environment in a way that will guarantee them a place in heaven?

3   We looked at a modern image of life after death on pages 36–37. The artist, Stephen Bird, showed hell as an underground concrete car park.

Draw or describe your own image of a modern hell. If it is a drawing, label the parts, taking care to explain why you think it is so horrible.

4   Look at the ancient Egyptian wall painting below. It shows the souls of the dead being judged by weight.

Identify:

- the person sitting in judgement
- the beast who will eat the bad souls
- the one writing down the results.

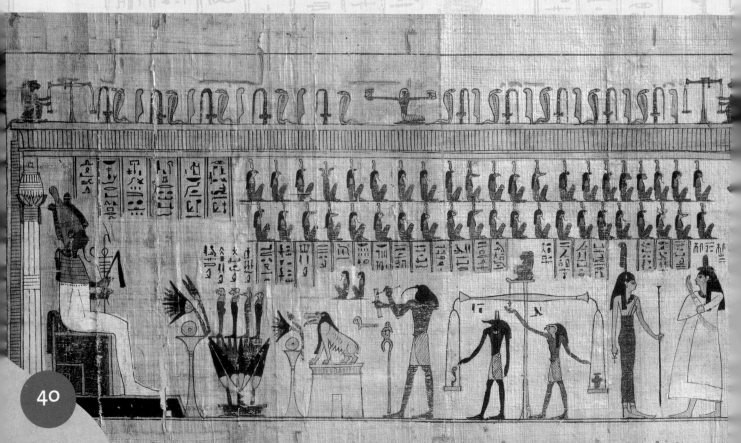

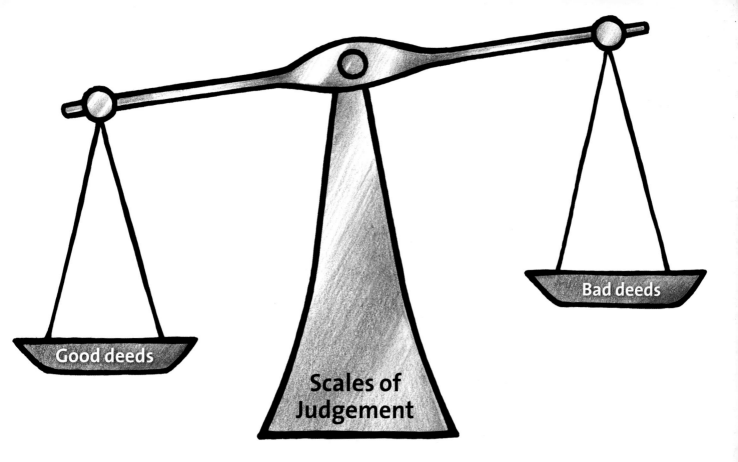

Good deeds

Bad deeds

Scales of Judgement

5 a *Individually or in pairs, list 10 bad deeds and 10 good deeds a person might do in their life. Against each, write how many plus points and how many minus points each action is worth.*

As you work, you will need to consider how each deed might balance against the other. Could some deeds outweigh others?

b *How many points do you need to score to go to heaven or to hell?*

6 *'You aren't punished for your bad deeds. You are punished by them.'*

a *Discuss what the difference is.*

b *Which view would a Christian accept?*

c *Who might believe in the other view?*

d *Would you agree with either or them? What would you say?*

7 *Produce a poster, story or poem to show: 'There is no such thing as luck – you get what you deserve.'*

8 *Write two sentences explaining why Christians think Jesus' Resurrection made such a difference to people.*

9 *Design two sympathy cards. One is for a Christian and the other for a Buddhist or a non-believer. What message and what image would you choose for each one to bring comfort to the person who receives it?*

Communicating by prayer

In this unit we look at prayer as a method of communication. We ask whether it works; how people get themselves in the right mood; and who they think might be listening.

The footballers opposite appear to be trying to contact God. Not everyone believes God exists, but these footballers' actions worried the opposition enough for them to ask for them to be stopped. Why should they want to stop this?

3.1 Consider the similarity between using your mobile and praying.

3.2 Look at how people get themselves into the right frame of mind.

3.3 Examine the differences between worshipping with others and alone.

3.4 Investigate who people might pray to.

3.5 Consider the Archbishop of York's strange camping experience.

3.6 Look at the way some people believe their prayers are answered.

How do you get in touch?

Let's look at the idea of prayer as simply a method of communication.

Asking for help

Even people who hardly use mobiles are likely to say they need one for emergencies. The elderly man whose car breaks down at night is grateful to have a mobile tucked in his pocket. The ramblers lost on the moors when the fog descends are relieved to discover there is a signal on their mobile. The 999 call can be a lifeline.

Maintaining friendships

For most young people a mobile is the most reliable way of keeping up with friends. Whether it is a chat or text, it is nice to know what is going on and to know somebody cares about you. Often the chit-chat can be meaningless, but the feeling of friendship is not.

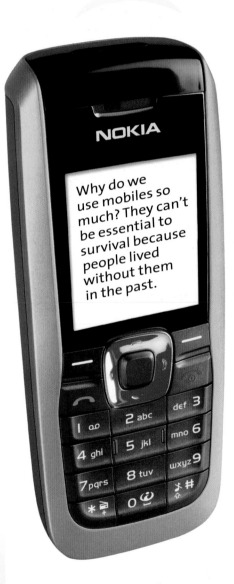

Why do we use mobiles so much? They can't be essential to survival because people lived without them in the past.

Keeping the family together

There used to be a BT advert urging us to 'ring round the family circle'. Although it is likely that most young people's calls are actually to friends, it is true that the phone can help to hold families together. A quick call to Mum ensures you get picked up after a school trip and lets her know where you are. Old people who live alone and some distance from relatives, find a phone call reassuring. They feel part of the family when they know what is going on.

Arranging events

Regular chatting can lead to get-togethers. Because people always keep their mobiles with them, it is easy to fix a time and place for meeting, right up to the last minute.

1 Study four adverts for mobile phones. For each advert, decide what the manufacturer is saying through its words or pictures about why you must have their product. Would any mobile do the same job?

> What has this got to do with prayer?

There is a remarkable similarity between using a mobile and praying. Both involve trust and belief. Using your mobile means you believe there is someone out there waiting to hear from you. It also shows you are expecting someone to send you messages, which you will be able to receive and act on.

When people pray it is much the same. They trust that God is able to receive their thoughts and will reply in some form. Believing someone is out there, even though you can't see them, is as much a part of modern life with emails, texts and voice mail, as it is of religion.

If you were to stretch this idea a bit further, you could say there are times when the signal is good and other times when you just can't get a signal.

2 Describe a situation when a worshipper might feel they 'can't get a signal'.

3 Draw your own spider diagram to show prayer is like using a mobile. Write 'God' in the centre and use the same four headings as in the diagram on page 44. Briefly say how each act might be applied to prayer.

Rising soul singer, Corinne Bailey Rae, makes no secret about her belief in God. Her method of communicating with God is through her voice. 'When I'm singing, I feel spiritually connected. I don't go to church at the moment but I have a bunch of people I grew up with that I see regularly and they feel like my church.'

(Source: The Times 27 January 2007)

Soul singer Corinne Bailey Rae

4 What question would you like to ask Corinne Bailey Rae about her method of prayer?

Remember

Prayer is a vital method of communication between God and people.

3.2 Getting focused

Getting into the right frame of mind is important for most things, but particularly when communicating with God.

> Are special preparations needed?

At first, it may seem strange to go through lots of preparations before making contact with someone, especially a supernatural power who probably isn't greatly concerned about human appearances anyway.

However, Muslims don't agree. For them, preparations are an important part of prayer. By undertaking a special washing ritual called wudu, Muslims are showing God that they want to be pure. Equally, following a set pattern of washing before prayer helps to calm the mind. This washing is not just a case of going through the motions, Muslims must give their full concentration to it and that helps them push aside busy thoughts.

> The place might help

Muslims face the direction of the holy city of Makkah to pray. The wall in the mosque that does this is called the qiblah wall. In this picture, it is shaped like an alcove and reminds Muslims that the ear of God is always ready to receive people's prayers. For prayers at home, a picture of the holy city of Makkah or words from the Qur'an might be placed to mark the direction of Makkah.

> Could special clothes help?

> I am Jewish. Putting on special garments helps me to make my prayer an important event, something out of the ordinary. It is commanded in Jewish scriptures that men should put on a hat, shawl and these leather boxes for morning prayer, so I obey. Each piece I put on has a special meaning which I focus on as I put it on. By the time I have finished, I am in the right frame of mind to focus on God and my prayers.

1 A Jewish man's hat is called a kippah, the shawl is a tallit and the leather boxes on the head and arm are called tefillin. Find out the meaning each has for a Jew.

> Do pictures or words help?

Some people get into the right mood by concentrating on words or pictures. These can get them on the right track. In Christianity, there may be pictures relating to an event in the religion's history or a statue of a holy person.

Words can be helpful. A Christian might read a piece of holy scripture or think about a saying that is written on the wall. The words can make a good beginning to the prayer or just provide something to start thinking about.

There are no set rules; people use whatever they find helpful in settling their mind and preparing them for communication with God. A flower or something from the natural world could start the worshipper thinking about God as creator and make them want to give thanks.

2 Give two reasons why a picture might help a worshipper. Why might somebody else think pictures and statues are a bad idea?

> Just do it!

Sometimes prayer is just spontaneous. The sight of a small baby might make someone say, 'Oh bless'. If there is an emergency situation where someone wants God's help, they'll just ask. No preparation is necessary for the 999 prayer!

3 Design a poster to show three different ways in which people prepare themselves for prayer.

To finish

4 What helps you to settle down and concentrate on your homework?

3.3   Your place or mine?

Here, we look at what people gain from worshipping with others and what they gain from worshipping by themselves.

Think about what the people here gain from being in a crowd. It's live, that helps! Whilst people do enjoy watching football at home on television, it can't compare with actually being there and soaking up the atmosphere.

1 *Draw a speech bubble in your book to show what the lady in the front of this crowd might say. Why will she say it is better to be at the match than at home watching it on TV?*

Surprisingly, taking part in a football match, as a member of the crowd or a player, has a lot in common with taking part in religion. Perhaps that is why some newspapers have called football the new religion!

2 a *Copy and complete the table below so you can decide for yourself whether you agree that football has a lot in common with religion. Add any more categories you can think of.*

b *Where do you think the comparison fails?*

	Football	Religion
Special clothes for those involved and the followers		
Special place		
A leader		
Special chants and songs		
A small group of people at the heart		

This congregation is taking a very active part in Christian worship at a Black Pentecostal church. Worshippers don't have to be black to attend, everyone is welcomed. The origin of this 'full-on' style of worship was the Caribbean, so the majority of the congregation are usually black and bring with them the vibrant traditions of their homeland.

Worship here is lively with loud joyful music and lusty singing. Traditional prayers are used, which members of the congregation join in with, and there is also an opportunity for spontaneous prayer. The minister may construct a prayer as he goes along and it is quite common for members of the congregation to call out their own contributions aloud.

Those who attend feel a strong sense of a living God who is in tune with his people. Worshippers gain great strength from being involved with others.

Communicating with God privately

Some people prefer to communicate with God privately. Another branch of Christianity concentrates on personal contact with God. When Quakers meet together to worship they sit quietly in a circle. For them, prayer takes the form of personal thought but they do like to get together to meditate. Occasionally, one of them may stand up and share their thoughts with the group.

Not everyone feels the need to have people around them. For some, it is more of a distraction than a help. Having a relationship with someone is intensely personal and communicating with God is no different. Alone, a person can relax and say whatever they want to God without fear of being overheard or embarrassed. Some like to begin with a set prayer and others use whatever words come into their head. Some people don't use words to pray at all – they just think in ideas.

3 *Design a leaflet the Black Pentecostal Church in the picture above can give to newcomers. It needs to tell newcomers about prayer and what a Christian might gain from joining in their worship. You could do some Internet research for more ideas.*

To finish

4 *Make a list of three things people gain from praying with others and three things people gain from praying on their own. Which would you prefer?*

Here, we investigate who people might pray to.

> Let's start with the obvious

God. Most of what we have been studying has been concerned with the way people try to make contact with God. As the highest possible power and creator of everything in existence, it is not surprising that most people turn to God for comfort and advice, as well as offering praise.

> Is it hard to approach such a great power?

Hindus offer prayers to God, the Supreme Spirit, through the elephant-headed figure of Ganesh.

We have all been in the position of wanting to approach someone really important but felt more comfortable asking a friend to do it for us. Some Christians choose to direct their prayers to people who have already died – people like saints, who once led holy lives on earth and are believed to be close to God in heaven.

1 *Find out why Ganesh is such a popular figure in Hinduism. Write a label that could go next to his statue telling people why they might like to offer prayers to Ganesh.*

> Using a go-between

Many Christians like to pray to Jesus. Not only was this Jesus' suggestion, but Christians feel the Son of God, who once lived on earth, will understand their problems best. Prayers often end with the words 'Through Jesus Christ, our Lord' showing that the worshipper is using Jesus like an ISP (Internet service provider) to pass messages on to God. The technical name for praying like this is intercession.

Roman Catholic Christians often pray to Mary, the mother of Jesus. Because she was human and a mother, they believe she will help them.

Remembering a beloved granny.

Some people think that a much-loved relative who has died is watching over them.

At times, their presence is felt so strongly, the earthly person believes they can communicate with them in their mind. You could say those thoughts are a form of prayer. Others would say that it's not prayer, it's just wishful thinking or an over-active imagination.

> Could it be all in the mind?

The idea of praying to a great power and receiving an answer could be in the imagination. If something occupies our thoughts a lot, our mind will be actively trying to come to conclusions, whether we are aware of it or not. When a believer comes up with the answer, they will thank God. But did they actually solve it for themselves?

Some would say that God is within everyone anyway. If he was going to help us find a solution, then he would put the answer in a person's mind.

MEMO

From: DJF Productions

Subject: HIGH PRIORITY – Thursday morning's show 'Talking it through with Diane'

Guests: Marc Lowton, famous psychologist who says 'It's all in the mind!'

Bishop Morton who has been urging people to join a week of prayer for peace at the cathedral.

Diane needs to get the guests talking about whether prayer really exists.

---

2 *Supply two questions that Diane can ask the guests to kick off the discussion. Give Diane a few tips on what they are likely to say in reply to her questions.*

Remember

Some people find it easier to communicate with God through another human who has died. That person will carry their prayer to God.

Here, we examine one person's prayers and consider what they have achieved.

> *What do you think is going on here?*

ARCHBISHOP'S CAMPING HOLIDAY

The Archbishop of York, Rev Dr John Sentamu, spent a week living in a small tent inside York Minster praying and fasting for world peace. He lived on water for seven days whilst his wife and children went off on their summer holiday.

God speaks through the BBC

Like many others, Dr Sentamu had seen television news reports of innocent people caught up in the conflict between Lebanon and Israel. More and more casualties were reported every day. Sentamu said that he did pray for peace but felt that wasn't enough. He didn't know how to answer the emails and letters that poured in from Christians asking what they could do to stop the violence. The turning point came when Sentamu listened to a BBC news report from a hospital in Lebanon. There, an eight-year-old girl had lost an eye in an attack, her parents and brother had been killed but no one had told her. 'It was like a bayonet went into my heart,' he said. 'It just got to me.'

Gutted

Another report from an Israeli village showed an 85-year-old woman abandoned as the villagers fled the bombing. 'She could have been my mother,' Sentamu said. 'I found myself so devastated. My prayers were just crying out to God. This was atrocious. I couldn't get it out of my mind.' He went on to say that he was 'gutted at the plight of the young and the elderly, at those who are helpless in this conflict. And then I realised this was what I had been trying to hear. I was hearing the voice of God in that little girl, in that old woman.'

Action called for

The Archbishop looked in the Bible for help. There, he came across a story where Jesus' disciples tried to heal a boy and failed but couldn't understand why. Jesus told them that it was prayer and fasting that were needed. That gave Sentamu the answer. Because most victims of war are forced to live in tents when their homes are destroyed, Sentamu decided to camp like them. The big difference was that Sentamu's campsite was the Minster church.

Ever hour between 9am and 5pm Sentamu held a seven-minute prayer service which was relayed around the Minster by a loudspeaker.

Adapted from: *The Sunday Times*, 20 August 2006

1 *Write a postcard home from a foreign visitor to the Minster who saw the Archbishop camping. What do they think about what they have seen?*

> Did it make any difference?

It is difficult to say. Sentamu's camping exploit certainly captured the headlines that week. Newspapers, magazines and television all reported what he was doing and the reasons. Messages of support flooded in. Tourists at the Minster joined in his hourly prayers, even though they had never thought of praying about the situation before. People wanted to give money to buy food and medicine for the victims of the war.

Rev Dr John Sentamu started his prayer vigil after Morning Service on Sunday and the next day a ceasefire was announced. 'The more I pray, the more coincidences there are,' was his reaction.

2 *Write a reply to the person who posted this comment on the Minster's website: 'I think his prayer protest is stupid. It's just a stunt to get attention.'*

Remember

God can speak to people in unexpected ways.

Believers are convinced that God does answer prayers but it may not be how people expect. Here are two examples for you to consider and make up your own mind.

'God moves in a mysterious way, his wonders to perform,' Christians sing in one of their hymns. How much is it mystery and how much just wishful thinking? When Archbishop John Sentamu began praying for peace on the Sunday, a ceasefire was declared the next day. 'The more I pray, the more coincidences there are,' he told reporters who wanted to know if it was a miracle.

1 *The Archbishop's words are very clever. What is he actually saying about the way God works?*

Below is another situation where you could say prayers were answered.

This grainy image of Norman Kember in captivity was broadcast on an Arabic TV station.

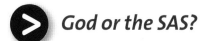

God or the SAS?

In November 2005, four Christians who did not agree with violence went to war-torn Iraq. They wanted to bring friendship and to reassure the people there that many people did not agreed with the attack on Iraq. Three days after the group had arrived, they were kidnapped and held hostage for 118 days. The American amongst them, Tom Fox, was murdered.

There was intense diplomatic activity to free the men and Christians and Muslims around the world prayed for their safe release. The men themselves prayed daily. Norman Kember, the 73-year-old English member of the group, admitted, 'God remained largely veiled during those months of captivity... We knew people were praying for us but there is evidently no simple relationship between prayer and answer.' On 23 March 2006, the SAS stormed the house and released the three survivors.

Norman Kember said, 'If God does answer prayer, he does it through the agency of the intelligence services and the SAS!'

2 *Norman Kember will be on the Breakfast Programme. Supply two questions you would like to ask him about his beliefs or the way his prayer was answered.*

Please give your own opinions about his prayers and his release.

> After my mum died I knew I ought to sort out her clothes and things. I didn't want to do it and I wasn't sure what I was going to do with them. As I was thinking about it, I could hear her voice in my head saying 'Take them to the charity shop'. So I did. Now you could say she was watching over me and helping. It seemed like it at the time. Now I think it was all in my mind. I knew her so well that, deep down, I knew exactly what she would have said if she had been here.

3 a *Would you say that this person's prayer was answered? Why?*

   b *What do Christians mean when they say God moves in a mysterious way?*

To finish

4 *Write a 150-word story about an incident where someone might say their prayer was answered and someone else might say it was a fluke.*

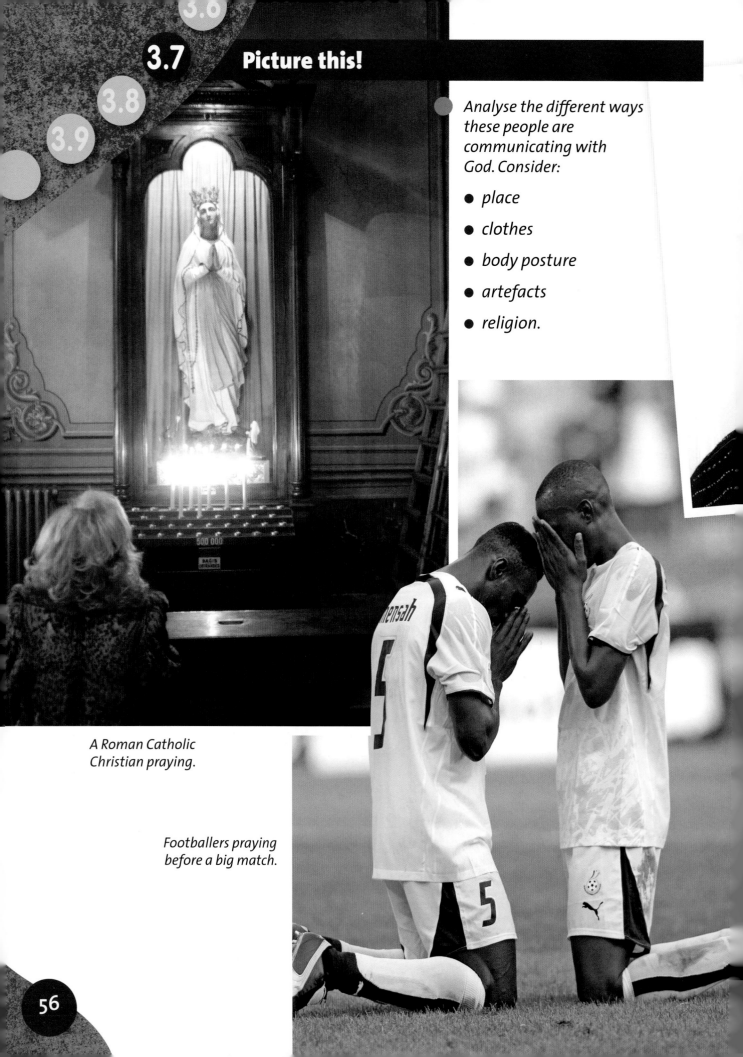

Analyse the different ways these people are communicating with God. Consider:

● *place*

● *clothes*

● *body posture*

● *artefacts*

● *religion.*

A Roman Catholic Christian praying.

Footballers praying before a big match.

A Sikh meditating.

A Muslim praying.

All through this unit of work we have been studying how people get in touch with God.

Write down three ways that immediately come to mind.

 Let's remind ourselves of what we have learned:

We began by considering the similarities between communicating with God and using a mobile phone. **A** Why do some people think prayer is a two-way thing? **B** When might a person make an emergency call to God?	**We went on to look in detail** at the way people get themselves into the right frame of mind for God. **A** State one thing a Muslim does to prepare for prayer. **B** What sort of clothes does a Jew put on for prayer?
We examined the different approaches to worship and the ideas people had about who might be receiving their prayers. **A** Who might a Roman Catholic pray to? **B** Who might a Hindu pray to?	**We studied specific examples of answers to prayers** and considered whether it might be God or wishful thinking. **A** Which was the most unusual answer to prayer you read about? **B** When might somebody say, 'It's not God answering your prayer, it's a fluke'?

28 2 2006
15:18:25

Can you remember what this person said about the way God answered his prayers? (Look back to page 55 if you need help.)

Choose one of these tasks to check your progress in this unit.

Task one

a *Describe two different occasions when someone might feel the need to pray to God.*

b *Give your thoughts on the advantages and disadvantages of praying in private.*

c *If someone asked you 'What do you mean by prayer?' how would you explain it?*

Task two

a *Describe the preparations a person might make before they pray, for example a Jew or a Muslim (or you can describe another faith).*

b *What do you think when people say they don't believe in God, yet, when faced with a life-threatening situation, they pray? Is this acceptable? Why?*

c *When people say God has answered their prayers, do you think it's all in their mind? Why?*

1 Archbishop John Sentamu said, 'One drop of water cannot turn a water wheel but many drops can.' What has this got to do with prayer? Display Sentamu's idea as a series of cartoons with captions explaining the meaning underneath, or as a poster.

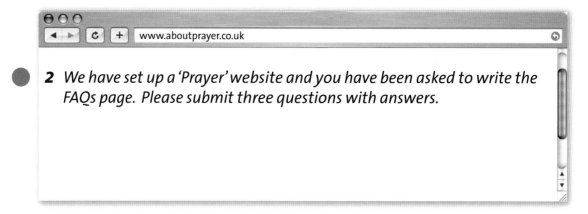

www.aboutprayer.co.uk

2 We have set up a 'Prayer' website and you have been asked to write the FAQs page. Please submit three questions with answers.

3 Design a poster called 'Communication'. Your aim is to show many different ways people believe they can reach God. In addition to ways discussed earlier, you might include dance, music, art, etc.

4 Some people might say that wishing someone well is similar to praying for them. With that in mind, what wishes or prayers would you make for a new baby? What would you wish or pray for when saying goodbye to a beloved friend who has died?

5 Consider what God might text in reply to someone who suddenly sends a 999 prayer, but who has never bothered to communicate with him before. Remember that in all religions God is merciful and forgiving!

6 Design your own room where you can relax or communicate with God. What atmosphere would you try to create and how would you do it? You can draw and label a diagram to show your ideas.

7 Complete an acrostic poem based on the word 'PRAYER'. Try to include something to show it involves two-way communication.

P
R
A
Y
E
R

8 *Write a label to go on the wall alongside this picture, explaining who this is and how some Christians may involve her in their prayers.*

UNIT 4 Forgiveness and retribution

Forgiveness is at the heart of what most religions teach to their believers. But, even if you are not religious at all, being able to forgive is one of the most valuable qualities you can have.

This unit will look at seven different aspects of forgiveness and then challenge you to come to your own conclusion about what you think.

4.1 Find out what is meant by forgiveness.

4.2 Examine what happens when people can't forgive.

4.3 Investigate the Christian idea of forgiveness.

4.4 Study an example of Christian forgiveness.

4.5 A case study of forgiveness.

4.6 Consider another religious response to forgiveness.

4.7 Understand why non-religious people think forgiveness is common sense.

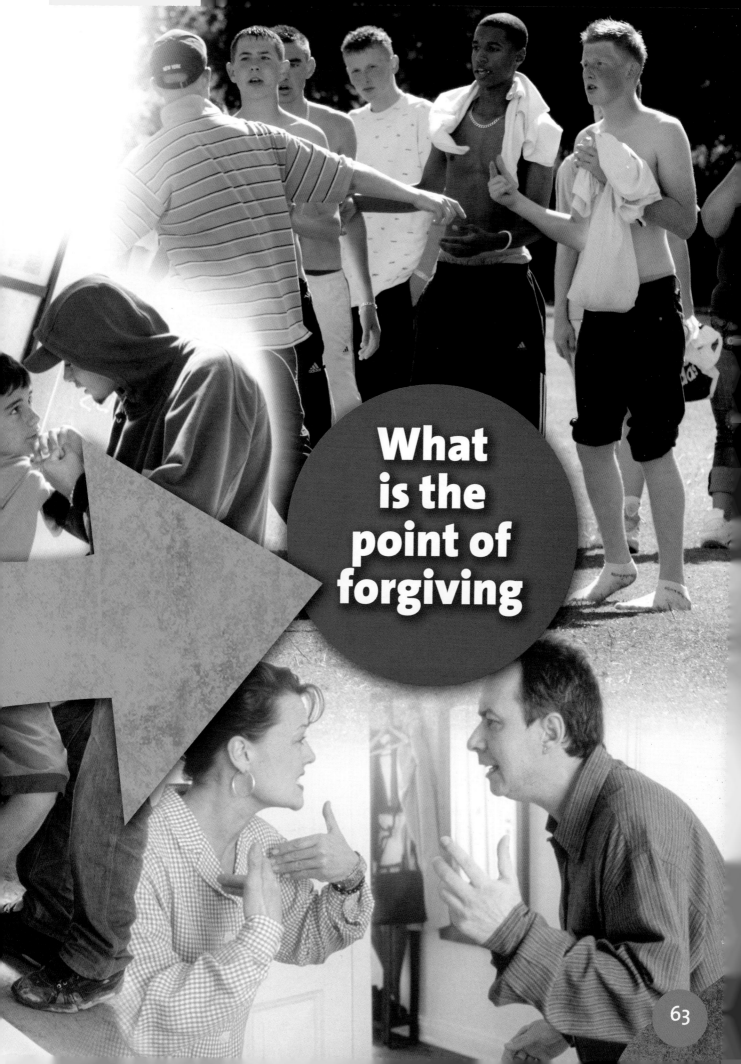

What is the point of forgiving

What do we mean by forgiveness?

When we talk about forgiveness what do we actually mean by the word? What is the point of it? Let's have a look at what is involved.

> Is it saying sorry?

Saying sorry is a part of forgiveness but it may not be the most important part. We can all think of an occasion when someone has muttered 'Sorry' when they have hurt someone and it is quite clear they aren't! They just think that if they say the magic word, it will get them off the hook. It does a bit, doesn't it? Getting angry with someone who has apologised is difficult. It makes you seem in the wrong.

> Perhaps it is a two-way thing?

The original action would have involved at least two people, so it will take both of them to mend the problem. One has to say sorry and the other has to accept this apology if things are to move forward.

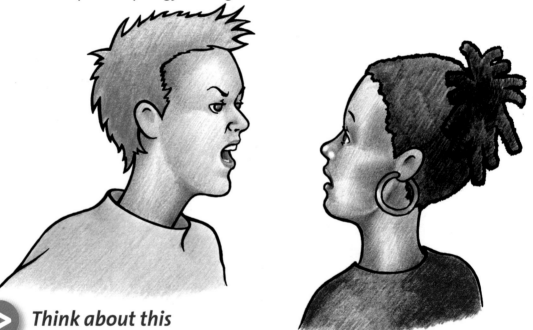

> Think about this

Chelsey dashed through the classroom at break and knocked over the chair where Craig had put his jacket. She didn't bother to pick anything up and ran across Craig's jacket without a second thought. He was furious and had a go at her. Chelsey just shrugged it off saying she was in a hurry. Her friend Paula said she ought to apologise because it was a new jacket. So Chelsey just yelled across the room, 'Sooorrry!' Craig was furious. He knew she didn't mean it and so he wouldn't accept it.

What everybody in this situation really wants to do is draw a line under the incident and get on with their lives.

1 *Play around with these ideas:*

| Chelsey says she is sorry | Chelsey does mean it | Craig says it is okay |
| Chelsey doesn't mean it | Chelsey refuses to apologise | Craig won't accept her apology |

Write each of these scenarios on a separate slip of paper. Try putting different ones together to see what effect they will have on the outcome. Which do you think is the best arrangement to get a peaceful outcome?

> Who is the strongest?

In a situation like this, one person usually gets the upper hand, often the person who inflicts the pain. There will also be a victim, the person who is hurt by the action.

2 *Who would you say has got the upper hand in the story of Chelsey and Craig? Why?*

> Who is the weakest now?

At first, the weak person is the one who gets hurt. Then the power shifts. The person who has to say sorry and ask to be forgiven is putting themselves at the mercy of their victim. What if they are turned down? Who has got the upper hand then?

3 *a Begin your own strip cartoon story, or write a story where someone hurts another.*

b If you have drawn a cartoon, colour the stronger person in red in each frame. If it is a story, underline the strong person's name in red.

c Continue your story to include one person saying sorry, and the other person accepting their apology.

d Decide who you should highlight in red at the end of the story.

e It is quite likely that, by the end, the power has shifted from one person to another. How has the victim ended up the strongest? What would have happened if the apology had not been accepted?

Remember

Forgiveness involves two people. One has to ask for forgiveness and another has to grant it.

4.2   What happens when you can't forgive?

Occasionally, somebody does something so awful that it seems impossible to forgive them. Look at the way one mother deals with a drunken driver who killed her teenage daughter.

FATAL ACCIDENT HERE

> I won't forgive him. He killed my Kylie. He was totally drunk when he got in that car. She was only 15. She had her whole life in front of her. I bet he only does three years inside. Then he'll come out and get on with his life. None of us can ever do that.
>
> But when he comes out, I'll be waiting for him. Doesn't matter how long it takes, I'll track him down and I'll kill him. I've got to do it for Kylie's sake.

1 *Draw a speech bubble in your book to show what you think Kylie might want to say to her mum.*

> How does Kylie's mum deal with this situation?

She has clearly suffered a terrible shock and hates the man who killed her daughter. This is perfectly understandable, most us would probably feel the same way. What she plans to do later is more questionable.

2 *List three reasons why you think Kylie's mum wants to kill the driver.*

We don't know if Kylie's mum said this in the heat of the moment and didn't really mean it. Maybe it was a carefully considered reaction. Do you think she will wait around for the driver to serve his time in prison?

Think of the hatred that will build up inside Kylie's mum. Think of the stress it will cause her. Her health will suffer and she won't be able to concentrate on anything else. What will happen to her friends? What will happen to her if she really does kill the driver?

3 *a* *Write the word 'HATRED' down the side of a page as shown below:*

Having sleepless nights for weeks on end
A
T
R
E
D

b *Use each letter to start the line of a poem that shows how hatred actually causes more suffering. The first line here has been given as an example only. The poem does not need to rhyme.*

> **At the start of this section we asked 'What happens when you can't forgive?' Here is one answer:**

A Chinese proverb says:

'Whoever chooses revenge should dig two graves.'

4 *Either:*

● *draw a cartoon to illustrate the Chinese proverb above*

Or:

● *try to explain the proverb's meaning to an eight year old. What example would you choose to help them understand?*

5 *Write down what Kylie's mum might have said when she heard the proverb? Do you agree with her?*

Remember

The person who can't forgive is likely to suffer the most.

What do Christians mean by forgiveness?

Christians, like many others, believe forgiveness is vital if we are all to enjoy a good life. They don't see it as weak or insulting. Jesus taught them a special way of looking at forgiveness and he set them an example.

What do you think this wise old saying mean?

'Do as you would be done by!'

'Come on, fair is fair!'

Yesterday, Simon Jenson was jailed for 18 months for stealing £25,000 from his boss, celebrity footballer Darren Poulter. In a statement Poulter said, 'When I first discovered what Jenson had done I was mad with him. I was going to get the police in. But he pleaded with me to go easy on him. He said his girlfriend was ill and he had been under a lot of pressure. So I forgave him for nicking my cash. I didn't even ask him to pay it back.

But what made me really mad was the way he treated his mate the next day. The poor bloke only owed him a tenner from the other week but Jenson landed him in hospital.

And after what I had done for him! That was the limit. The least he could have done was show a bit of charity to the poor guy!'

1 a *Some people said Poulter was too lenient on Jenson. As a class, decide whether Poulter should have been harder on Jenson. Would that have changed things?*

   b *Who do you think is the hero of the story and who is the villain? Why?*

2 *Write a report for the evening paper stating what Poulter said to the press outside court or what Jenson told the jury about his behaviour.*

Poulter's story is a modern version of a story Jesus told in Matthew 18:21–35.

When he finished the story, Jesus said it gave us an idea how God would treat us if we didn't forgive people. If we don't forgive, then God won't forgive us for our wrong doings at the end of our lives. We will be punished.

It is more than just saying sorry

What was revolutionary about Jesus' ideas was that he said you should go out of your way to be kind to the person who hurt you. It's more than just accepting their apology.

3 *What did Poulter do that was extra generous?*

A line in the prayer Jesus taught Christians to use says:

'Forgive us the wrongs we have done, as we forgive the wrongs that others have done to us.' (Matthew 6:12)

4 *In the story about the celebrity footballer, who represents God? How do you know?*

Jesus wasn't all talk. Look at the way he put his words into action.

Even when Jesus was dying in agony on the cross, he prayed for the people who had nailed him there. 'Father forgive them, they do not understand what they are doing,' he told God.

Remember

Jesus taught that it is essential to forgive people who harm you. God will judge you on the way you have shown forgiveness to others.

4.4   How can anyone deal with this sort of thing?

When a whole country has been hurt and many of its people have committed atrocities, forgiveness seems impossible. Look at the way one Christian set about solving the problem.

> Here is the problem:

For over a hundred years South Africa was ruled by white people, even though most people were black. The white government ruled by force and deprived black people of their rights. Black people had a very low standard of living, poor education and menial jobs. In 1994, things began to change and Nelson Mandela became the country's first black president. He set up a new government with people of all colours, religions and races.

Terrible atrocities had been committed over the previous years. White people abused black people and black people retaliated with vicious attacks on whites. If the new South African government was to succeed, the past had to be laid to rest. There could be no more grudges, vendettas and settling of scores.

> How do you solve this problem?

Some people said, 'It is all in the past, forget it. Look to the future.'

Others said, 'No, that won't work. We need to round people up, hold trials and execute everybody who is guilty.'

● *1 In pairs, decide what the good and bad points of these solutions are.*

Nelson Mandela agreed that they must not ignore the terrible things of the past, but he thought that big show trials and executions would do more harm than good. He came up with an alternative: the Truth and Reconciliation Commission, known as the TRC.

> The new way

The new way was called 'truth' because people were asked to come forward voluntarily and tell the public about crimes they had committed. In exchange for telling the truth, no matter how terrible it was, that person would be granted an amnesty. This meant they would not be punished for the crime they confessed. Standing up and telling everyone what they had done was punishment enough.

Victims were also asked to tell everyone what had happened to them. Once the full truth was known, they could be given help. In fact, many victims said that just having people prepared to listen to their story went a long way towards helping them to recover.

2 *Draw a diagram to show the three ways Mandela considered for dealing with the horrors of the past.*

> Who could lead the TRC?

Archbishop Desmond Tutu is a Christian who was chosen to lead the TRC. He believes everybody is one of God's children, no matter what race or colour.

Nobody questioned or cross-examined anybody who spoke about their crime. Everyone just listened. This led to most people telling the truth because they were not frightened of interrogation or punishment.

> There is no future for South Africa without forgiveness. Revenge will lead to a blood bath. Forgiving and forgetting will allow South Africa to move forward.

Reconciliation meant everyone had to accept what had happened in the past and not seek revenge. Families discovered what had really happened to loved ones who had vanished or been murdered. Although it was terrible to hear, learning the truth helped them move on with their lives.

3 *Draw a poster that the TRC could pin up on a village notice board. It needs to tell people what the TRC is going to do and why people should help its work.*

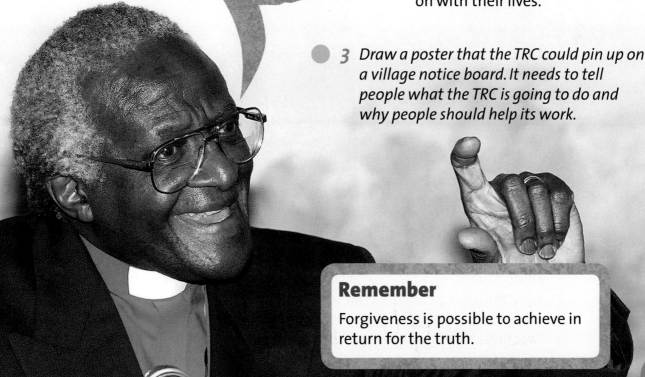

Remember

Forgiveness is possible to achieve in return for the truth.

They said it wouldn't work!

No country had ever tried to deal with the terrible events of the past in the way described on pages 70–71. Many said it wouldn't work. 'The Kleenex Commission,' people sneered, because many witnesses were in tears as they told their story. On these pages are two cases the TRC heard.

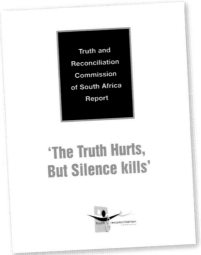

Truth and Reconciliation Commission of South Africa Report

'The Truth Hurts, But Silence kills'

1 What does the motto on the TRC's pamphlet mean? You can give an example if you like.

CASE 1

> ### How would you treat a person who blinded you?

Neville Clarence (on the right) was blinded in an explosion in the city centre of Pretoria. 21 people were killed and over 200 injured when the car bomb, planted by Aboobaker Ishmail (on the left), exploded outside the headquarters of the South African Air Force.

After listening to Ishmail's account of what he had done and his apology for hurting so many, Clarence asked to go over to him. Although he was blind and had never had any compensation for the accident, Clarence said, 'I have absolutely no grudge whatsoever to bear, never have and never will, against the perpetrators of that car bomb explosion.'

The two men shook hands as Clarence forgave Ishmail. It was very emotional for everyone present.

Aboobaker Ishmail shaking hands with Neville Clarence at the TRC.

CASE 2

> ### What is it like to carry guilt around?

Policeman Brian Mitchell ordered his men to kill members of a political gang. That was bad enough, but the orders got muddled. In December 1988, 11 innocent villagers, mainly women and children, were massacred.

Mitchell was found guilty of their murder and sentenced to 30 years in prison. He was haunted by the horror of what he had done and asked to appear before the TRC to admit his crime. After he confessed, he asked the village to forgive him. 'I have lost everything in life,' he said. He was in prison, his wife had divorced him and his son wanted nothing to do with him.

The villagers agreed to forgive him on the condition he worked to rebuild their community.

Arrangements were made for Mitchell to go to the village. He was scared because many hated him for killing their relatives. By the end of his first visit, warmth and understanding were beginning to appear on both sides.

   2 *Choose one of these case studies and write, or role play, a radio interview with a victim and the perpetrator.*

> ### Did the TRC work?

The TRC has brought peace and reconciliation to South Africa. It is true not everybody has been able to forget the horrors they suffered and some wanted revenge, but the predicted blood bath never happened.

The world has watched the South African experiment with interest. There has been talk of using a similar approach to heal the scars of Northern Ireland's violent past.

Following Jesus' teachings, Archbishop Tutu has always looked for the way of peace and non-violence. He accepts that it is normal for people to feel anger and hatred at what has happened, but he wants people to 'hate the sin but love the sinner'. What is the difference?

   3 *Look back to pages 68–69. Find one way in which Archbishop Tutu's approach to forgiveness matches Jesus' teachings.*

> **Remember**
>
> The TRC successfully used the Christian idea of forgiveness.

An eye for an eye?

Not everyone shares the same approach to the problem of forgiveness. Here, we consider a Jewish way of dealing with forgiveness.

Some people say 'An eye for an eye and a tooth for a tooth' is the right way to respond to someone who hurts you.

1 *Draw a large outline of an eye and, inside, explain what 'An eye for an eye' means. Beneath, write reasons why some people say this is a good solution.*

2 *This was what the famous Indian leader Gandhi said. What did he really mean?*

> An eye for eye, soon the whole world will be blind.

> One Jewish response

The 'eye for an eye' principle is important to Jews. They believe it is perfectly natural to be angry if somebody hurts you. People who hurt you should not be allowed to get away with it by just saying sorry and assuming that is the end of the matter. Punishment is an essential part of justice, Jews argue. The expression 'An eye for an eye' comes from Jewish scriptures and is in the Old Testament. It means that a person who does wrong must pay the exact price for what they have done – but no more. Once this has happened, the matter is over.

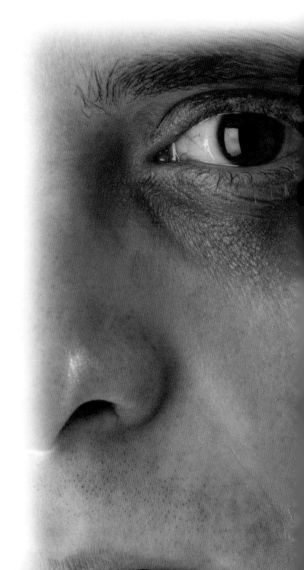

This response to hurt was an improvement on the bad old days. What used to happen was that one bad deed was often repaid with a worse one. Then the other side retaliated and, before long, a vendetta had begun. By stating that one injury would be repaid by an equal one prevented the violence from escalating.

3 *What would you say to someone who says, 'An eye for an eye is the fairest way out'?*

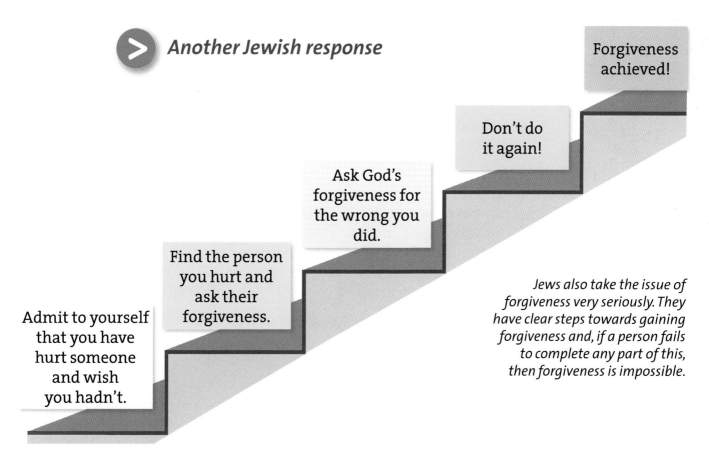

Forgiveness achieved!

Don't do it again!

Ask God's forgiveness for the wrong you did.

Find the person you hurt and ask their forgiveness.

Admit to yourself that you have hurt someone and wish you hadn't.

Jews also take the issue of forgiveness very seriously. They have clear steps towards gaining forgiveness and, if a person fails to complete any part of this, then forgiveness is impossible.

Notice that the person who has done wrong has to ask for forgiveness twice before they can be truly forgiven.

4 *Which of the four steps do you think is actually the hardest? Why?*

5 *If the person began on step 2 and got to the top, they would not gain God's forgiveness. Does this seem fair?*

> Making a fresh start

To show how important forgiveness is, Jews set aside a special time of the year. During the 10 days of Rosh Hashanah, which is the Jewish New Year, Jews think about unkind words and actions they have done during the past year. Once a person has accepted they were in the wrong, they must try to find the person they hurt, apologise and ask for forgiveness. It can involve doing something to show how genuinely sorry they are for the unkindness.

The person who has been hurt should try to grant forgiveness. Only when this is done, can a Jew turn to God and ask forgiveness for their sins on the tenth day.

To finish

6 *Write two sentences explaining how the Jewish idea of forgiveness is different from the Christian one. (You can remind yourself about this on pages 68–69.)*

Here, we look at how two people dealt with the difficult issue of forgiveness and the outcome.

Jo Berry's father was an MP, murdered in a bomb attack on the hotel where he was staying for the Conservative Party Conference in 1984. The bomber, Pat Magee, was a member of the IRA. He received several life sentences for his part in the killings but was released in 1999 as part of a deal called the Good Friday Agreement.

Jo says, 'It felt as if a part of me died in that bomb. I was totally out of my depth but somehow I held on to a small hope that something positive would come out of the trauma. So I went to Ireland and listened to the stories of many remarkable and courageous people who'd been caught up in the violence. For the first time, I felt that my pain was being heard.'

In November 2000, Jo took the daring step of contacting the bomber. 'I wanted to meet Pat to put a face to the enemy, and see him as a real human being. At our first meeting I was terrified, but I wanted to acknowledge the courage it had taken him to meet me.'

Pat Magee agreed to meet Jo because he wanted to explain why he had got involved in violence. He said, as a nineteen-year-old, he had seen his small community mistreated by the British and believes no one should 'just lie down and take it'.

Although they will never agree about the use of violence, Pat and Jo have steadily worked at getting to know

Jo Berry with Patrick Magee, the man who killed her father in a bomb attack.

An IRA bomb destroyed The Grand Hotel in Brighton, killing and maiming many people including Jo's father.

each other and understanding the other's point of view.

Jo says, 'I'm beginning to realise that no matter which side of the conflict you're on, had we all lived each other's lives, we could all have done what the other did.'

Pat says, 'I am 100% in favour of the peace process, but I am not a pacifist and I could never say to future generations anywhere in the world, who felt themselves oppressed, "Take it, just lie down and take it".'

 ## What good has come out of this?

Since they met, Jo and Pat have worked together promoting alternatives to violence.

1 *Write a blog for Pat Magee.*

Jo has formed an organisation that works for world peace called 'Building Bridges for Peace'. Jo and Pat sometimes appear together at conferences and also work separately. Both are committed to working towards a peaceful world.

When Jo first spoke on television about forgiving the man who had killed her father, she was accused of betraying her father.

2 *Compose the email Jo sends to her critic, giving her reasons for forgiving Pat Magee. (You might wish to remind yourself about Kylie's mum on page 66.)*

To finish

The Dawson Committee awards medals for courage. There are suggestions that one of the people in the story on these pages should be nominated.

3 *Give the Dawson Committee your recommendation on which of the two people shown on these pages showed the greatest courage and why.*

Picture this!

Rev Julie Nicholson.

The Rev Julie Nicholson's daughter,
Jenny, was murdered in the London
tube bombings on 7 July 2005.
She can't forgive the killer and has
problems being a vicar.

Jenny.

When the Americans bombed Trang Bang in Vietnam with a Napalm bomb on 8 June 1972, this nine-year-old girl lost everything – her clothes, her family and her village. Years later, the American pilot who dropped the bomb wanted to meet Phan Thi Kim Phuc to ask for her forgiveness. She forgave him.

Phan Thi Kim Phuc as an adult after years in hospital and 17 operations to repair the terrible burns to her body.

4.9 Just to recap

All through this unit of work we have been asking 'What is the point of forgiving?' Write down how you answered this question at the start of the unit. What new ideas have you gained from this study?

> **Let's remind ourselves of what we have learned:**

We began by deciding what the word 'forgiveness' actually meant. Forgiving somebody is closing an episode. We found out that it did not mean being weak and backing off. Quite the opposite. The person who forgives comes out on top.

A Why should anyone bother with forgiveness in an argument?

B How can the person who forgives come out on top?

We considered what happens when a person won't forgive and found that it caused them even more pain.

A How does a person who can't forgive suffer?

B Why do they say forgiveness is a two-way thing?

We looked in detail at the Christian idea of forgiveness and then went on to see if it worked in action.

A What's different about the way Christians think of forgiveness?

B Why do Christians think it is important to show forgiveness?

We went on to examine the Jewish approach to forgiveness and examples of forgiveness that had no religious basis.

A Why do Jews think 'an eye for an eye' is the best way to deal with forgiveness?

B When is the special time of the year for Jews to think about forgiveness?

Can you remember what was unusual about Archbishop Tutu's treatment of murderers and rapists in South Africa? (Look back to page 71 if you need help.) Why was his approach successful?

Choose one of these tasks to check your progress in this unit.

Task one

a What did Jesus say people should do if they were hurt by another person? Give one real-life example of where this was successfully put into practice.

b Do you think this approach could work in most situations? You will need to give some examples (real or imaginary) to explain this.

c If someone asked you, 'What's the point in forgiving people?' what would you say?

Task two

a Why don't Christians think forgiveness is weak?

b Why do some people find it hard to forgive, and what happens when they can't?

c Would you say that forgiveness is always the right thing to do? Why?

AN EYE FOR AN EYE

YOU HAD IT COMING TO YOU

All's fair in love and War

It's dog eat dog

GIVE AS GOOD AS YOU GET

GET IT OUT OF YOUR SYSTEM

TiT FOR TAT

Forgive and Forget

Remember and Resent

FAIR IS FAIR

Kiss and Make up

● 1 *a* *Choose two graffiti statements you disagree with above. Explain what they mean and why you think they are wrong.*

   b *Copy the graffiti statements on to slips of paper. With a partner, sort them into two categories. Those statements that you think will lead to peace and those that you think will make the situation worse. Put any statements you can't agree on in a third category.*
   Join with another pair to compare your results.

● 2 *Make up an acrostic poem using the letters from the word 'FORGIVENESS'.*

LOVE IS......
NEVER HAVING TO
SAY YOU'RE
SORRY.

F
O
R
G
I
V
E
N
E
S
S

3 On the left, Oscar Wilde and Nelson Mandela are both telling people to say sorry, but for different reasons. In what way do their reasons differ?

4 In the cartoon at the bottom of page 82 is a popular line from an old film.

   a Think about the saying and decide what was meant by it. Do you think it is true?

   b Is saying sorry and asking for forgiveness an important part of a personal relationship? Why?

5 'The Forgiveness Project' is a non-religious organisation that believes forgiveness is a vital ingredient in world peace.

   a Look at their website (www.theforgivenessproject.com) and read more about Jo Berry and Pat Magee's story that appeared on pages 76–77.

   b Investigate another real-life story featured on the website and report back to the class.

Can you forgive murder?

On Tuesday 3 October 2006, a 32-year-old truck driver burst into an American schoolroom armed with knives, guns and 600 rounds of ammunition. He sent the boys out then began shooting the girls. He massacred five before turning the gun on himself.

The strict Christian Amish community in Pennsylvania were stunned. They live a simple life without modern appliances and believe in peace and non-violence. They have no guns, no cars, no police and no security systems.

Putting Jesus' message of forgiveness into practice, they forgave the gunman. 'There is no sense in getting angry,' one said. 'We want to forgive. That's the way we were brought up – turn good for evil.'

One member of the community immediately went to comfort the wife and family of the gunman. The Amish have also set up a fund to help his family.

6 Read the article above. Do you think the Amish community did the right thing?

5 Rituals and routines

In this unit we ask whether it is any help to have a routine or a pattern to the way we go about our daily lives. We look at the way people celebrate events and examine religious routines.

5.1 Consider whether there is anything to be gained from doing the same thing over again.

5.2 Examine the reasons for celebrating certain events in our lives.

5.3 Think about what people gain from celebrating the same festival every year.

5.4 Consider the advantages of having set words to recite.

5.5 Investigate the reasons people go on pilgrimage.

5.6 Look in detail at the Muslim pilgrimage to Makkah.

Are patterns any help?

Is there anything to be gained from doing the same thing at the same time over and over again?

> Boring

Doing the same thing day after day, or year after year, sounds boring with no one making any progress. There is some truth in that. Imagine having to wear exactly the same design of clothes every day, including weekends and holidays. That would be worse than a school uniform! It wouldn't do us any harm, but most of us would get fed up with it and long for the chance to choose for ourselves. We want to be able to express our own personality.

> All change!

Do you ever feel life is like this? You are put in a lane and you just have to keep on running with no freedom to break out. Look at it from another angle. It is careful adherence to the routines learned in training that enables athletes to achieve spectacular results.

Imagine what it would be like if there wasn't a school timetable. You would come to school each day and have no idea what lessons you would have. It might be a bit of a laugh to begin with but then it would be a nightmare. You would never have the right things with you for the lesson, so time would be wasted. Not being in the right frame of mind for what was coming would also mean you didn't make as much progress as usual.

You have only got to think about when you go to a new school to realise how unsettling it is. Everything is new, that's tiring. You are always on the alert, keeping your eyes and ears open so that you get to the right place at the right time and don't miss something vital. That saps your energy before you even start a lesson.

Settling into a routine can be quite liberating. It means all the boring basics are sorted out and you don't have to give them a second thought. You are free to get on with what matters.

When it comes to religion, the same can be true. As we have already discovered, what matters most to believers is making contact with God. When people are able to do this, they benefit from knowing how to behave and they feel cared for.

1 *Children in Need events come round every year. Design a flier for one of these events telling people to support it. Add something to counter any criticism that it is yet another boring old money raiser.*

2 *Draw a spider diagram with the word 'Family' in the middle. Write boxes around this central word showing the different things a person gains from being part of this same group of people all their life. Things to consider are reassurance, support, etc.*

3 *List all the routines a member of a religion might have in their life. Think about festivals, prayers, worship, etc.*

Remember

Having set routines to follow can help people to feel comfortable and grounded. This frees them to go on and reach new heights of achievement.

Let's look at the reasons why we celebrate certain events in our lives, even though they are perfectly normal.

Some people might think that if events come around regularly like clockwork, most of us will ignore them. When it comes to birthdays they are wrong! We all look forward to our own birthday which is strange because it is so predictable. Everybody has one as well, so why is yours special?

1 *List four reasons why your birthday isn't just another boring routine for you. Does it matter to anyone else?*

> Why are some personal events more important than others?

It is true that we all enjoy a birthday, and our own most of all, but some events in our lives have more significance than others.

2 *Draw a timeline for Jo Bloggs, from her birth through to her death as an elderly lady. Mark six points on her timeline when you think she would have had a special celebration to mark that stage. Under each point, give a brief reason why it was such an important time for her.*

> Moving from child to adult is a big leap

Some people would claim this is the most significant point in your life. Certainly eighteenth birthday parties can be wild events! Many religions also think it is important to mark this stage in someone's life. It is the time they become an adult and take responsibility for themselves, their actions and the consequences.

Who is the coming of age ceremony really for? Is it for the person concerned? You could say no, because the date in the calendar will come round whether they do anything or not. Also, it is unlikely they will wake up that morning feeling any different to how they felt the day before. You might say the ceremony is for everybody else's benefit.

3 *Design an invitation to a coming of age party. Inside the card tell people why it is important they attend this event.*

> Marking the step to adulthood in Judaism

A Jewish boy comes of age at 13 years. Does this seem too young to you? Before the age of 13, the father is responsible for his son's behaviour and for making sure his son does the correct things. After 13, the boy must take full responsibility for himself.

is is the highlight of a Jewish boy's coming of age ceremony. He has to stand up in public and read from the scrolls in Hebrew.

4 *What would you set as the best age for becoming an adult? Give two reasons.*

In the year before his thirteenth birthday a Jewish boy learns about the religious duties he will have as an adult. He also learns more about his religion and studies enough Hebrew to read the scriptures in their original language. On the holy day after his birthday, he will read a passage of scripture aloud in the synagogue. Scary stuff! Everybody present can see that he has now come of age and will treat him as an adult member of their community.

To finish

5 a *Design your own ceremony to mark the fact someone is now to be treated as an adult.*

Things to think about:

- *Do there need to be any special preparations?*
- *Will there be any sort of test to prove they are now an adult?*
- *What will happen on the day?*

b *Explain your ideas to the class in a poster, or produce a leaflet to tell young people coming up to adulthood what they must do.*

5.3 Oh no, not Christmas again!

Here, we examine what people gain from celebrating the same festival year after year.

Like birthdays, Christmas comes round once a year. Unlike birthdays, there is nothing personal about Christmas; quite the opposite! The festivities only work really when people get together. Usually, this means family but often friends are involved as well.

1 *Draw a large speech bubble in your book saying: 'Oh no, not Christmas again!' Inside, write why a person might say this.*

2 *In another speech bubble, write what someone else might say to this person whom they think is a spoil-sport.*

> ## If you forget all the hype, what's left?

Christmas is exactly what it says it is. It is a mass, or festival of Christ, and for Christians this is hugely important even if they don't do any extra shopping. The birth of the most important person in the religion, as Jesus is for Christians, is certainly worth celebrating. Look at this diagram to see why Christians think their annual festival is worthwhile.

Remembers major events in the religion.

Makes the group stronger.

Why are festivals important to Christians?

Passes the stories on to the next generation.

Strengthens a person's beliefs.

Is a time when people feel closer to God.

Good excuse for a celebration!

Brings family and friends together.

3 Draw a larger version of the diagram on page 90 in your book. For each bubble, write a sentence to explain exactly how a Christian puts each point into practice at Christmas.

> ## If you aren't a Christian, you shouldn't celebrate Christmas

This sounds a bit like Scrooge but, occasionally, people say it. They argue that if you don't believe in Christ, there is no point in going to his birthday party. You wouldn't gate-crash somebody else's party. Do you agree?

4 Research how Hindus or Sikhs celebrate the festival of Divali. Find two similarities and two differences with the way Christians celebrate Christmas.

> ## What is gained from a festival that comes round every year?

The answer all people give is that it keeps the religion alive. Stories get forgotten unless they are passed on. Most of us lead such busy lives we don't have time for storytelling once we are out of babyhood. At festival time, traditional stories are often incorporated into songs (like Christmas carols), plays (like nativity plays) and scenes appear on cards. All this keeps the story alive and teaches the next generation.

This is a scene at the Hindu and Sikh festival of Divali. Like Christmas, this festival comes round once a year and worshippers look forward to it eagerly.

Reminding worshippers of the event they are commemorating can help to bring them closer to God. This strengthens their belief. Being amongst a large number of other worshippers at festival time can create such a special atmosphere that people feel more in touch with each other and God.

To finish

5 Prepare an email explaining why your family will be celebrating Christmas. They can be religious or non-religious reasons. If your family does not celebrate Christmas, explain why.

Let's look at what people gain from reciting the same words over and over again.

Why do groups enjoy singing the same songs when they get together? It is much the same as the way friends share a joke when they get together or greet each other with the same words. What do they gain from doing this?

> ### What if those words came from someone special?

Supporters' groups and fan clubs often use the same expressions as their hero. It helps them feel closer to him or her and helps the group bond better. The same is certainly true of religious followers. The words are often profound and when people repeat them, they gain more insight into the true meaning. If the words are believed to be those of God, they take on an even greater significance.

1 *Can you think of a cult TV show or film that produced some popular sayings? List a few words or phrases you know friends use when they meet. What do you think they gain from this?*

This group of Sikhs are quietly chanting the word 'Waheguru' to themselves. The word and its rhythm combine to free up the worshippers' minds to concentrate on God.

> ### You can lose yourself in words

Sometimes we don't follow what is being said and get lost, but it is also possible to repeat set words over and over again so you drift away. The words become a means of escaping from the real world. Sikhs use the word 'Waheguru', meaning 'Wonderful God', as a way of meditating. Gentle repetition of this word helps a Sikh to settle their mind and become more in touch with God.

All the religions have favourite prayers that worshippers know by heart. You might think words would lose their meaning when someone knows them so well they could say them in their sleep. The opposite can happen. Reciting familiar words is reassuring and helps to settle the mind. Another advantage of using a liturgy, as these set prayers are called, is that it frees the mind to concentrate.

Think about when you are trying hard to read something, or to remember exactly what you are being told. All your attention is taken up with the effort; you don't bother with the meaning. How different it feels when you can just drop into something familiar.

> ### The Lord's Prayer
>
> Our Father in heaven
> May your name be honoured;
> May your kingdom come;
> May your will be done on earth as it is in heaven.
> Give us today the food we need,
> Forgive us the wrongs we have done,
> As we forgive the wrongs that others have done us,
> Do not bring us to hard testing
> But keep us safe from the Evil One.

This prayer is regularly used by Christians because Jesus taught it to his followers. It has the advantage of containing everything a Christian might want to say to God in one easy form. No need to search around for ideas, nor worry about forgetting things.

2 *Copy down 'The Lord's Prayer' in your book and underline in different colours the words that express the following:*

- *Praise.*
- *Confession.*
- *Asking for help.*

Don't forget to add a key.

Remember

Some people find it helpful to have set prayers to use in worship. It makes them feel part of a group and frees their mind to concentrate on God.

Here, we examine what people gain from going on a pilgrimage to a well-known place with set rituals.

> *A pilgrimage or a holiday?*

There is a difference between going on holiday and going on a pilgrimage, even if people end up at the same place. Examining their motives will help us to understand the difference. The tourist's main aim is to enjoy themselves, whereas the pilgrim's aim is to get closer to God. This doesn't of course mean pilgrims won't enjoy themselves as well, but it certainly isn't their main intention.

> *Choosing the place*

There are always special places in any religion. These are usually where something important happened in history. Page 114 shows the cave where Muhammad was given the words of the Qur'an. Standing on the spot where something actually happened can be a powerful experience. It helps a person to feel more connected to their history, whether the place is the sight of an ancient battle or a religious experience.

1   *Name three places where something happened in the past – they do not need to be religious. Which site would you most like to visit and why?*

This site is sacred to Christians because the silver star on the floor is believed to mark the spot where Jesus was born in Bethlehem. For this reason, it is an important pilgrimage destination where Christians go to pray and feel closer to the central figure in their religion.

Joining the crowds

Because they are such significant places, religious sites are often crowded with other pilgrims but this can be an advantage. Joining with lots of like-minded people can be exhilarating. You have only got to look at the crowds at a pop concert or football match to see the strength of feeling people get from being together. For pilgrims, it is the same. They are enveloped in a powerful sense of belonging which often makes spiritual connections easier to establish.

Freedom

Being in a holy place, away from everyday concerns, is liberating for many people. They no longer have to worry about what they must do at what time and so on. Instead, they can focus totally on God. Following in the footsteps of other pilgrims, past and present, visiting a holy site and stopping to pray at the same points they did, helps worshippers to feel part of a strong group. That's powerful.

From the Memorial Garden at Yad Vashem, pilgrims walk into a hall that is lit by five candles. Their light is multiplied using mirrors to create a starry ceiling. Each star represents the soul of a child who died and in the background can be heard the names of the children being quietly recited.

Shown above is a slightly different place of pilgrimage. Here, you can see the feet of people visiting Yad Vashem, a memorial to the one and a half million Jewish children murdered by the Nazis in the Second World War.

2 *How is the Children's Memorial at Yad Vashem different from other pilgrimage sites? What do you think pilgrims might do there?*

To finish

3 *Design a leaflet that could be given to a religious group advertising a pilgrimage. You can choose the destination. It might be one on these pages or another well-known shrine. You will need to include details of why this site is important and how a pilgrimage to this place might strengthen faith.*

Because the pilgrimage to Makkah depends a great deal on set routines and patterns, we need to consider what Muslims gain from going.

One of the five most important duties in Islam involves a pilgrimage to the holy city of Makkah in Saudi Arabia. This pilgrimage is called Hajj in Arabic. A Muslim must try to go on Hajj at least once in their lifetime. Hajj requires a large commitment of time because a pilgrim will spend at least a week in Makkah and more likely two. It also costs a lot of money.

 ### Going at a set time

Although it is perfectly possible for a Muslim to visit Makkah at any time of the year, the holy pilgrimage of Hajj can only take place during one particular month. This means that Muslims from all over the world gather for Hajj. This involves two to three million people coming together during the month to worship God in the same place at the same time.

 ### Wearing set clothes

On arrival at Makkah, pilgrims change into simple white cotton robes, called ihram. By removing all signs of wealth and culture, pilgrims feel united and equal. This frees them to forget about themselves and concentrate totally on God.

When Muslims drink water from the well of Zamzam, they are remembering that God will provide all that is needed for us to survive as he did in ancient times.

Following a set route

Pilgrims begin by walking around the Ka'bah, the site of the first ever place of worship, which stands in the middle of the Great Mosque at Makkah. Crowds attend most days. After circling the Ka'bah seven times, pilgrims begin a set trail which will take them several miles around holy sites.

Performing set rituals

At certain points on their journey, Muslims perform rituals. It might involve throwing pebbles at three stone pillars, having their hair cut, running along a walkway or standing and praying on a particular hill. As they concentrate fully on the action, they are reminded of a similar episode in history and the power of God, then, and now, in people's lives.

1 What do Muslims gain from wearing the same clothes on Hajj?
2 What do Muslims gain by going on Hajj at the same time as everyone else?
3 What do Muslims gain from going to this particular place?
4 Research the story of Hajar and her connection with the well of Zamzam.

On return

Most Muslims returning from Hajj feel their life has changed. The pilgrimage is challenging, so completing it for God is a great achievement. Taking time out of daily life to concentrate totally on the spiritual, strengthens

Remember

By carefully following all the rituals of Hajj, Muslims are able to draw closer to God than they would in everyday life.

5.7 **Picture this!**

Jewish holy site at
the Western Wall
in Jerusalem.

Choose one of these pilgrimage
sites. Find out what a pilgrim
does there and why.

Buddhist holy site
at Bodhi Gaya.

*Skih holy site at
Amritsar.*

*Christian holy site at the
Sea of Galilee.*

5.8 Just to recap

All through this unit of work we have been asking whether it helps us to have routines and patterns in our lives. We have looked at the reasons why people celebrate birthdays and religious events.

 Let's remind ourselves of what we have learned:

We began by thinking about the advantages and disadvantages of doing the same thing day in day out. A What sort of routines do some religious people have? B What might be the disadvantage of sticking to a routine?	**We looked in detail** at what people gain from celebrating the same festival every year. A Name two major festivals Christians celebrate? B Who celebrates Divali?
We considered the advantages of having set rituals in worship. A What is the name of the most important prayer Christians recite? B Name one ritual Christians have as part of their worship.	**We went on to examine** in detail the reasons for going on pilgrimage, and particularly the rituals and routines of Hajj. A How is a pilgrimage different from a holiday? B Name one special thing a Muslim does on Hajj.

Write down what you thought about having a set routine when we began this study. Do you still think the same now you have finished this work? Why?

Poppy Day, or Remembrance Sunday, is part of an annual ritual. Why is it helpful to have it as a regular event?

Choose one of these tasks to check your progress in this unit.

Task one

a Give two reasons why people hold special events to celebrate a coming of age.

b Explain how one faith group celebrates a major festival.

c What is your view of other people celebrating a major festival when they don't belong to the religion?

Task two

a Give two reasons why people like to have set prayers they can recite rather than make up their own.

b Explain why some people go on pilgrimage.

c How would you answer those who say a pilgrimage is just an excuse for a holiday? You will need to give some examples from one of the religions to support your case.

There are lots of rituals in this ceremony. Why?

1 Look at the picture above. What two things does it achieve? In your opinion, is it worth doing every year? Why?

2 Using the word 'PATTERN' or 'ROUTINE' compose your own acrostic poem to show how members of a religion benefit from it.

3 Prepare a travel agent's brochure for pilgrimages to a religious site. You can choose which religion and which site to cover. The leaflet will need to include:

- where the place is and why it is holy to the religion
- any special preparations pilgrims will need to make before they go
- what will happen when the pilgrims get there
- what the pilgrim will gain from this journey.

4 What is the difference between a tourist and a pilgrim?

5 Write an entry for 'The Lord's Prayer' for Wikipedia, the online encyclopaedia. If you want to remind yourself of 'The Lord's Prayer', look back to page 93.

6 The Children's Memorial shown on page 95 is at Yad Vashem in Israel. It is a well-known pilgrimage site for Jews.

   a Look at Yad Vashem's website to find out what other memorials are there.

   b Produce an A4 leaflet explaining what pilgrims might gain from going there.

   c Consider what Christians might also gain from a pilgrimage there.

7 Design a T-shirt that could be sold to pilgrims returning from Hajj. Muslims do not like to see drawings of people, so avoid these in your design but make sure the T-shirt is meaningful.

8 Choose two religious festivals from different religions. Display their differences and similarities as a Venn diagram.

9 Find out more about the service of Holy Communion or Mass that Christians celebrate regularly as part of their worship.

   a What important event are they remembering?

   b What does the wine symbolise and how is it used in the ceremony?

   c Find out what the bread reminds Christians of and how much of it they eat. Present your findings as a poster or a short talk to the class.

UNIT

6

Sacred texts

In this unit we think about why books are so important to religions. Then we go on to find out why some books are holy and others just ordinary. This leads us on to examining what is in some holy books and how members of that religion use them.

6.1 Weigh up the difference between using a book and an electronic form of communication.

6.2 Consider what makes a book holy.

6.3 Examine why Christians believe the Bible is an exceptional book.

6.4 Look at the use of the Bible in public and private worship.

6.5 Find out how Muslims received their holy book.

6.6 Examine the way the Qur'an is used and respected.

Do you want that in writing?

Let's consider what books have to offer when compared with modern electronic forms of communication.

Few people would dispute that there are lots of advantages to using modern electronic gadgets. You have only got to think about how useful your mobile phone is, or all the things you can do if you have got a laptop computer. Because of this, drivers are increasingly fitting satellite navigation systems into their cars to make it easier to find their destination.

> *Whoops!*

Sat navs do make mistakes. You hear weird stories of drivers being told to turn into roads that don't exist or arriving outside a private house when they wanted to go to the hospital. What can a motorist do if he suddenly lands up in the wrong place because his sat nav has led him astray?

1 *Make a list of four different ways our driver can find out how to get to his destination. Rank them in order putting the most reliable first.*

   It is quite likely that high on your list of solutions will be looking at a map book.

2 a *Look at the way a book is being used in each of the four pictures below Think how it could be replaced by electronic technology.*

   b *What improvements would electronic technology bring? Do you think the situation would lose anything?*

 ## Are books dead?

It is certainly true that electronic wizardry has huge advantages over books, but there are some occasions when using a book adds something extra. Most religious groups have a book at the heart of their faith. The book was often written hundreds of years ago but is still being used today. All of these holy books now exist in an electronic format too. Maybe it doesn't matter whether it is in book form or on a screen. It is what it says that is important.

Advantages of a book

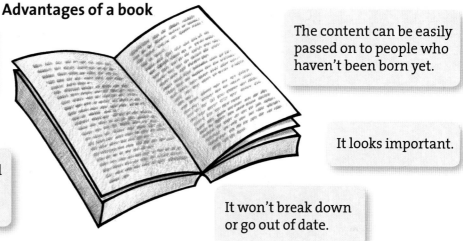

The words are recorded forever – they can't be changed or tampered with.

The content can be easily passed on to people who haven't been born yet.

It looks important.

It can be carried and used anywhere in the world. Batteries not needed!

It won't break down or go out of date.

 ## A book gives authority

In the situations shown in the pictures, most of us would feel happier if a book was used rather than a laptop. It gives the occasion a greater air of authority. There is always the fear that something recorded on a computer may get tampered with. The message may get hacked into, a virus might corrupt it, and then there is always the risk of the information being deleted by mistake.

In the past, when there was no electronic technology, books were a handy and reliable way to record information to pass on. Today, they remain at the heart of the world religions.

3 *Why do you think someone might appreciate a handwritten note that says, 'I was so sorry to hear your friend has died' more than a text that says the same? Or don't you agree?*

To finish

4 *Write two sentences to explain why books still play an important part in the life of twenty-first-century world religions.*

6.2   This one is different

Let's find out what it is that makes one book holy and another ordinary.

You could hardly call this an ordinary book. Hundreds of people queued up to buy the next volume of Harry Potter when it went on sale at midnight. That has never happened with any book before.

HARRY POTTER
and the Half-Blood Prince

BOOK LAUNCH 16TH JULY 01.00

SPECIAL OPENING HOURS SATURDAY 16th JULY 01.00 - 07.00 - 07.00

1 If you asked someone in the queue why they had stayed up all night to get this book, what would they say?

> Is it a best-seller?

It is true that most holy books are best-sellers, though nobody ever publicises the fact. In an average year, 44 million copies of the Bible are sold worldwide. That has to rank as one of the top best-sellers of all time. Even sales of the latest *Harry Potter* book, or any other popular best-seller, never sells anything like that amount.

> Does it have to be expensive to be special?

Strangely, money doesn't actually come into it. You certainly can see incredibly beautiful copies of holy books that are very rare and handwritten. Their covers may well be encrusted with precious stones, but that doesn't make them holy. It makes them very expensive when they come up for auction though, but it is the fancy trimmings that are fetching the money, not the words inside.

2 *Think about the value of this photograph album? Write down two reasons why this album is worth nothing to you and two reasons why it is priceless to descendants of the family shown here.*

> **What makes a book holy?**

It is a best-seller. Lots of people all around the world have copies.

The holy book contains rules for daily living as well as stories and songs with meanings.

People treat the book with more respect than any other book.

Study of a holy book will change a person's life.

The contents of the book are the most valuable part of it. A battered paperback would be just as holy as a hand-bound diamond-studded copy.

The way the holy book came into existence is different to other books. The words have been inspired by God. In some cases, they are thought to actually be the words of God.

To finish

3 *Write a reply to this magazine letter:*

'I have just paid the earth for a first edition of Harry Potter and the Order of the Phoenix. *I think it is pretty special. This book has been a mega best-seller and my edition was seriously expensive, so why isn't it a holy book?'*

6.3   Why is the Bible special to Christians?

Christians hold the Bible in high regard. Here, we look at why they believe this book is completely different to any other.

In the previous section we thought about the reasons why people believe a certain book is holy. To remind yourself of those reasons, look back to page 109. Now we are going to look in detail at the reasons Christians give for treating the Bible in a special way.

>   Where did the Bible come from?

This is not an easy question to answer because the Bible is actually made up of 66 short books. They were written down at different times, in different languages and by different people. To make things more manageable, Christians divide the Bible into two parts. One part they call the Old Testament (which has 39 books in it) and the other the New Testament (with 27 books).

>   So who wrote them then?

The earliest books are over 2000 years old and most of the authors are unknown, but a few have given their names to the books, such as John and Amos. But it is not the name of the writer that makes the book special, it is the belief that God was behind the words.

I am sure the Bible really does contain the exact words of God. God put those words into the minds of chosen people and they wrote them on paper. It means everything in the Bible must be true – word for word.

Ben

No, I don't agree with that. The Bible is a book written by people. Okay, they were pretty special people because God inspired their writing but, let's face it, they were human beings. We all make mistakes sometimes. God's ideas? Yes, but the words they used were their own. That's the reason why some bits of the Bible contradict each other. And don't forget the people who translated it and wrote copies of the Bible. Mistakes probably crept in there accidentally. So, I would accept the general ideas but not everything word for word.

Jane

1 You are the producer of the Sunday show on Radio Donbury FM. Ben and Jane will be this week's guests. Write a memo to Steve, the presenter, so he knows what to expect. Explain that Ben and Jane are Christians and state what they disagree about and why.

Is it the content of the Bible that makes it special?

Christians find the Old Testament section of the Bible interesting because it tells them about their history and the part God played in it. There are also handy hints for daily life, like how to treat a skin disease or how to sterilise your plate if the dog has licked it! But it is the prophecies about Jesus that really matter to Christians.

A prophesy is a piece of information explaining what will happen in the future. The Old Testament contains several passages that state God will send his Son to save humans from their sins.

Enter Jesus!

The first four books of the New Testament, called the Gospels, tell Jesus' life story. During his lifetime, Jesus taught people about God and gave guidance about how they should live their lives. Because Christians believe Jesus was the Son of God, these books are the most important in the Bible. It is not just rules for people to follow but a real-life example of how Jesus behaved in difficult situations.

2 After last week's Sunday show, Radio Donbury FM's website has received this email. Please answer it.

Send Now Send Later Save as Draft Add Attachments Signature Contacts Check Names

From: John@talktalk.com
To: Steve@DONFM.com
Sent:
Subject: Sunday show

Size [Medium]   B I U T

Liked your show, Steve. But I don't get why an old book – and, yes, over 2000 years old in places – is of much use to Christians today.

John

6.4 How do Christians use the Bible?

Here, we look at some of the ways Christians use their holy book, both in church and in their private lives.

The Bible is very versatile, which is one of the reasons why it is still popular in the present day. Christians can use the Bible when they meet up with other Christians or they can read it on their own.

> Using the Bible with other Christians

Christians meet together for worship usually in a church, but some groups prefer to meet in each other's house. Short passages from the Bible are often read aloud for people to listen to and think about. Other pieces are incorporated into prayers or sung to music. The person leading the worship, who would be the vicar or priest in a church, is likely to talk in detail about one passage and explain its meaning to those listening. This helps Christians to understand how God wants them to live.

> The Bible takes a central part in ceremonies

The ceremonies families and friends attend to mark the important milestones in life involve the Bible. Appropriate passages are read aloud to welcome a baby into the community, to welcome an adult into the church or at a wedding or a funeral. Some passages give advice to those involved and others offer comfort to the listeners.

> Personal use of the Bible

Some Christians read parts of the Bible at home, especially passages dealing with Jesus' life. It helps them to get to know Jesus better and grow closer to him and to God, his Father. People faced with problems in relationships perhaps turn to the Bible to see how people in the past dealt with such things. Times might change but people don't. They still love, hate, make mistakes and become jealous, etc.

Worship

Guidance

Communication with God

Authority

What do Christians gain from using the Bible?

Problem solving

Comfort

Inspiration

1 Look at the four pictures below and decide which words surrounding the bubble on page 112 best suit each picture.

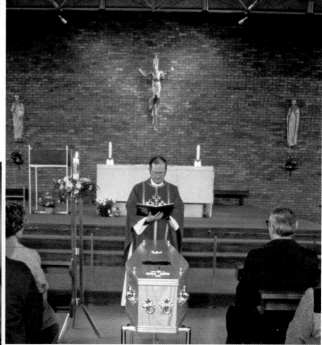

> ### Seeking advice

Some Christians use the Bible to help them solve everyday problems. They might look to see if Jesus was faced with a similar situation, or whether he gave his followers advice about it. Even the Old Testament, written hundreds of years ago, contains good advice.

2 Choose one of the following old biblical sayings and make up a story or design a storyboard to give its meaning.

   a 'A rich man has to use his money to save his life, but no one threatens a poor man.'

   b 'Discipline your children while they are young enough to learn. If you don't, you are helping them to destroy themselves.'

   c 'A gossip can never keep a secret. Stay away from people who talk too much.'

   d 'Getting involved in an argument that is none of your business is like going down the street and grabbing a dog by the ears.'

To finish

3 Design a bookmark to go inside every new Bible that is sold. Mention three ways a Christian could use their book. Use drawings instead of words, if you prefer.

6.5   Why is the Qur'an special for Muslims?

Here, we discover why Muslims treat their holy book, the Qur'an, with great respect.

> ### How did Muslims receive this holy book?

In the year 610 CE Muhammad saw an angel. The angel said, 'Read in the name of your Lord who created!' Muhammad was terrified and said, 'I can't read'. Three times the angel told him to read and, eventually, Muhammad found he could recite the words the angel told him.

Muhammad thought he was going mad but he told his wife what had happened. She realised the angel brought words from God and that it would be Muhammad's job to pass them on to people. This meant Muhammad was a prophet, or messenger of God.

Over the next 23 years, Muhammad received many visits from the angel Jibril with messages. He learned each one by heart carefully, then told his close friends who wrote them down. It was always read back to Muhammad to check for accuracy. After the final messages, the writings were put together in a book called the Qur'an. 'Qur'an' means 'recitation' because that was how Muhammad learned it.

1   *Write an alternative caption to this picture explaining why Muslims might like to go here.*

Here is the cave where Muhammad was sitting when he received the words of the Qur'an. Today, it is a holy site Muslims visit for prayer.

How can Muslims be sure the words haven't changed over the years?

Muslims believe the Qur'an contains the exact words of God. This is because God told the angel, the angel told Muhammad, Muhammad told his friends and the words were written down. There was no chance for mistakes to creep in.

Because Muhammad received the words from the angel in Arabic, they were written in that language. Today, Muslims who want to know precisely what God intends learn to read in Arabic even if they normally speak English or another language. Translations of the Qur'an exist and can be helpful but translations are never accepted as the real thing. That's because meanings get changed a bit when you translate from one language to another.

All written copies of the Qur'an are checked meticulously to make sure no mistakes ever creep in. If you check a modern Arabic edition of the Qur'an against the earliest handwritten one, it is word for word the same.

2 *Why is the Qur'an more important to Muslims than any other book?*

Recite this!

As well as copying the writing carefully, Muslims memorise passages. From age four, children learn by heart pieces of the Qur'an to use in prayer. Some people have also learned to recite the whole book by heart, just like Muhammad did. It is not just a great feat of memory, it is also a spiritual experience. If you first learn something by heart, you then gradually begin to understand its meaning.

Boys, some as young as nine, take part in an international competition to recite the whole Qur'an from memory. The annual award in Dubai began in 1996 and now attracts around 80 contestants during the month of Ramadan. Contestants have to begin their recitation at any point chosen by the judges.

3 *Design a leaflet or poster to advertise the International Holy Qur'an Award in Dubai. Include useful information about the language used, what the contestant will gain from the experience and what they have to do.*

> **Remember**
>
> Muslims believe the Qur'an contains the actual words of God. For this reason, it is more important to them than any other book in existence.

115

Here, we consider how Muslims use the Qur'an and the way they show respect for their scriptures.

> ### *Rules for life*

Muhammad explained to his followers that the book God had given them contained everything that was essential for life. It states they should worship only one God and gives them a set of rules for daily life. The rules in the Qur'an are correct forever, they will never go out of date.

> ### *Is it possible to have rules that never go out of date?*

It might seem unlikely because there have been so many new discoveries since the Qur'an was written down in the eighth century. Today, advances in technology get faster and faster. The Qur'an could never say anything about Internet fraud or designer babies because the technology for these hadn't been invented. But, actually, the problems are as old as the hills.

Fraud is telling lies and cheating people. Whether a person tells a lie to someone's face or texts their mobile, makes no difference. The Qur'an is clear about the fact that cheating is wrong and the person who does it will suffer.

Designer babies may seem more difficult until you read in the Qur'an that God is the creator of life. This means that nobody else can 'play God' and alter cells to create the sort of human being they want.

a Ryan lent his mate Steve the money to buy an ipod and Steve promised to repay it in a month's time. Steve now reckons he hasn't got the money. What should Ryan do? He feels let down because he trusted Steve.

b On Saturday, Charlene and Tracy were shopping when they saw a lad from their class on the other side of the road. Tracy yelled a daft comment across and told Charlene to do the same. It was just for a laugh. Should Charlene do it?

c Paul has been asked whether he would recommend his cousin for a job at the Sports Centre. What should Paul say? He knows his cousin was sacked for shop-lifting once before, but he is family after all.

1   Read the quotations from the Qur'an below. Find the ones that offer the best solutions to the three problems at the bottom of page 116.

'Be kind to your parents and the relatives and the orphans, and those in need and speak nicely to people.' (2:83)

'Whenever you speak, speak justly even if a near relative is concerned.' (6:152)

'Practise forgiveness, command decency and avoid ignorant people.' (7:199)

'Be modest in your behaviour and lower your voice. Truly the harshest of all voices is the voice of the ass.' (31:19)

'If the debtor is in difficulty, grant him time until it is easy for him to repay. If only you knew it, your repayment would actually be greater if you cancelled the debt.' (2:280)

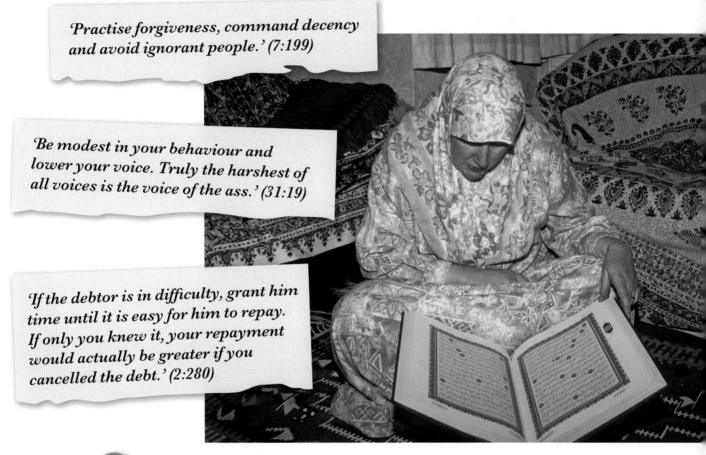

> Respect for the holy book

Because Muslims believe the Qur'an contains God's word, it is no ordinary book. Before it is used, a Muslim washes to show their respect for God's word. The book is always kept off the floor and often read on a little stand. When it is stored, the book is wrapped in material and kept on a high shelf. There, it will be safe from damage and the height shows nothing is above the word of God.

To finish

2   'The Qur'an is an old book, how can it possibly have any use in the twenty-first century?'

How would a Muslim answer this question?

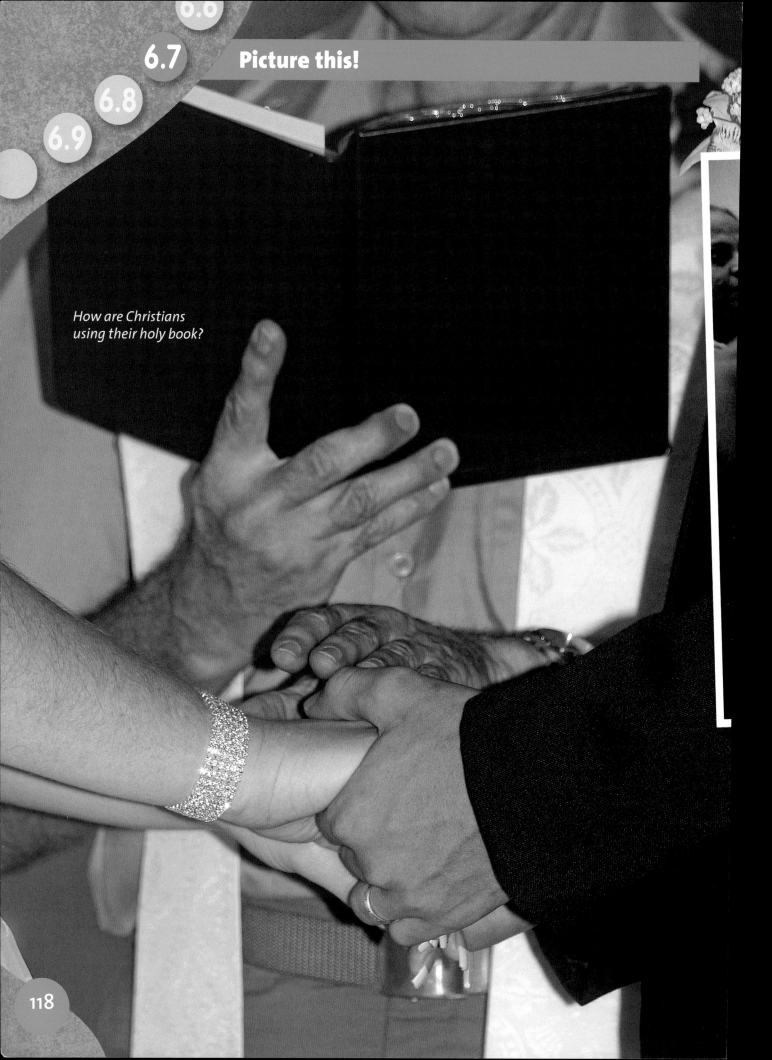

*How are Christians
using their holy book?*

Holy scriptures are used at all the important ceremonies in life. Look at the two ceremonies shown here. What do the people listening to them gain from the experience?

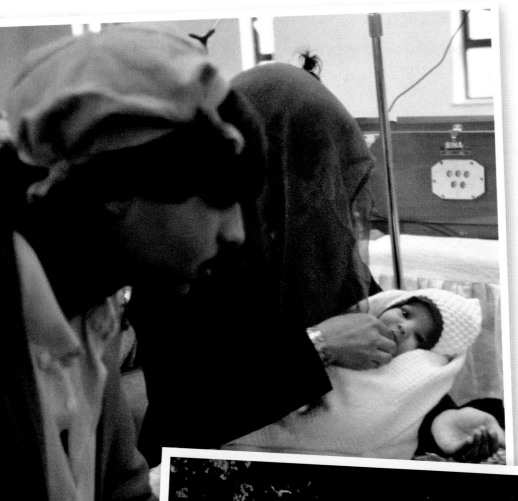

Sikhs choose a baby's name using their holy book.

The Sikhs' holy book, the Guru Granth Sahib, is opened at random. The letter that begins the text at the top of the left-hand page is given to the parents. They will choose a name beginning with this letter.

All through this unit of work we have been looking at people's attitudes towards holy writings and the way in which they use them.

Write down the reasons a member of a religion might give for saying 'I want that in writing!'

> **Let's remind ourselves of what we have learned:**

We began by looking at the way a book has more authority than many other forms of communication. **A** Give one reason why a book might be better than electronic forms of communication in some cases. **B** Give one situation from everyday life where a book is always used.	**We went on to find out** what it is that makes one book holy and another ordinary. **A** What is the name of a Muslim's holy book? **B** What is the name of a Sikh's holy book?
We looked in detail at Christian attitudes towards the Bible and the way they use their holy book. **A** Why do some Christians believe every word in the Bible? **B** Why do other Christians say you do not have to believe the Bible word for word?	**We examined** Muslim beliefs about the origins of the Qur'an and the effect it has on their daily life. **A** Where do Muslims believe the Qur'an came from? **B** Give one way in which Muslims show respect for the Qur'an.

At the start of our study many of you may have thought that a book that was hundreds of years old would be out of date. Now that you have completed the work, have your views changed at all? Why?

Here, you can see one way in which a book is being used at a marriage ceremony. How is the Bible used in this ceremony?

Choose one of these tasks to check your progress in this unit.

Task one

a Why do Muslims believe the Qur'an is the word of God?

b Not all Christians agree that the Bible contains God's words. Why don't some believe this?

c What difference do you think it would make if the Bible was totally replaced with electronic technology at church funerals?

Task two

a Describe two ways in which a Christian might use their Bible at home?

b Why do people say that a book about how we should behave will never go out of date? Do you agree?

c If the registrar at your wedding just typed the details into a laptop and never wrote them in the official register book, would you feel cheated? Why?

1 a Give everybody four post-it notes to build up a Wall of Wisdom. On each post-it note, everyone writes a favourite saying. It might be something your parents say; a line or two from a song; or just something you have heard and like.

   b When everyone has completed their post-it notes, display these on the wall. Words of wisdom and favourite saying like these are found in many sacred texts.

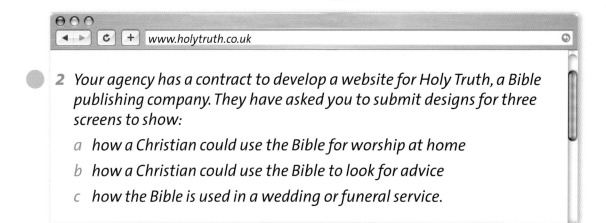

www.holytruth.co.uk

2 Your agency has a contract to develop a website for Holy Truth, a Bible publishing company. They have asked you to submit designs for three screens to show:

   a how a Christian could use the Bible for worship at home

   b how a Christian could use the Bible to look for advice

   c how the Bible is used in a wedding or funeral service.

3 Design a poster that a Muslim could put on the cupboard where they keep the holy Qur'an. The poster needs to tell people how the Qur'an must be stored and why.

4 On page 123 is a picture of a Sikh reading from their holy book called the Guru Granth Sahib.

   a Research three ways in which Sikhs show respect for their holy book.

   b Write a caption for this picture to give the viewer some idea of what is going on and the reasons.

5 Design a cover for a DVD that contains readings from one of the holy books. You can choose whichever religion you like. Before you consider drawing any people on the DVD cover, check whether members of that religion would be offended by drawings of humans on the cover.

6 Draw a cartoon or tell a story that involves a situation where someone says, 'I want that in writing!' Try to show why it is so important in that situation for the facts to be written down.

7 Explain how Sikhs use their holy book, the Guru Granth Sahib, to choose the name of a baby.

S
C
R
I
P
T
U
R
E

8 Complete an acrostic poem based on the word 'SCRIPTURE' that contains ideas about why these writings are special.

Glossary

A

Agnostic A person who is not sure whether or not God exists.

Amish community A group of people in America today who lead a very simple life without modern conveniences, according to Christian principles.

Amritsar The holiest city for Sikhs where the Golden Temple is situated. It is in the Punjab region of India.

Archbishop Desmond Tutu A black South African Christian leader who successfully led a non-violent campaign against black oppression in his home country. He is admired around the world for his work.

Atheist A person who is convinced God does not exist.

Atrocities Terrible sufferings inflicted on people by other people.

Authority A source of guidance on religious behaviour.

B

Bar Mitzvah The coming of age of a Jewish boy at 13 years.

Bethlehem The town in Israel where Jesus was born. It is a major place of pilgrimage for Christians.

Bible The holy book for Christians which is a source of authority.

Big Bang Theory A scientific theory which states the earth was formed as a result of a cosmic explosion. This is widely accepted.

Black Pentecostal Church A Christian group which has a lively form of worship based on Caribbean culture.

Bodhi Gaya The place in India where the Buddha reached enlightenment. It is a major place of pilgrimage for Buddhists.

Brahman The name Hindus give to God, the Supreme Spirit.

Buddhism One of the six major world religions. Buddhists do not believe there is a God.

C

Christmas The Christian festival to celebrate the birth of Jesus.

Creation story A story which has been handed down in a religion to explain how the world began.

D

Darwin's Theory of Evolution An explanation of the way humans evolved from apes. This explanation, first worked out by Charles Darwin, is now widely accepted.

Day of Judgement A moment at the end of the world when God will weigh up people's good and bad behaviour to decide whether they are to be punished or rewarded.

Designer babies A modern medical procedure which would enable a couple to choose the sort of baby they will have in terms of sex, hair colour, etc. This is very controversial because it involves destroying foetuses that do not match the couple's requirements.

Designer God The idea that everything in existence has a purpose because God deliberately made it that way.

Divali The Festival of Light, which is celebrated by Hindus and Sikhs.

DNA A scientific code which all living beings have. It has been called the pattern of life. Each one is unique to that being.

E

Everlasting life The idea that when a person's body dies, there is a spiritual part of them which will continue to exist forever.

G

Ganesh The Hindu God with the body of a person and the head of an elephant.

Gospels The four books in the New Testament part of the Bible that tell the life and teachings of Jesus. These are the most important scriptures for Christians.

Guru The name given by Sikhs to a holy teacher.

Guru Granth Sahib The name of the Sikh holy book.

H

Hajar The wife of the Islamic prophet Ibrahim. Her experience in the desert is remembered on the pilgrimage Hajj.

Hajj The Muslim pilgrimage to Makkah, which every Muslim must try to complete once in their lifetime.

Hinduism The oldest of the six major world religions. Hinduism began in India.

Holocaust The name given to the persecution of Jews, and others, by the Nazis during the Second World War.

Holy Communion A sacred ceremony for Christians which involves eating bread and drinking wine to remember the life and death of Jesus.

Humanists A group of people who do not believe in God or any religion but have a moral code based on respecting people as fellow human beings.

I

Ibrahim An important prophet in Islam. He is called Abraham by Jews and Christians.

Ihram White clothes worn during the Muslim pilgrimage Hajj to symbolise that everyone is equal in the eyes of God.

J

Jerusalem A holy city for the three religions: Judaism; Christianity; and Islam.

K

Ka'bah A holy site in the centre of the Prophet's mosque in Makkah. Muslims face in the direction of the Ka'bah when they pray.

Karma The idea that everything we do in life has consequences for us in this life or in a future rebirth. Buddhists, Hindus and Sikhs believe this.

Key to life An understanding of the meaning of life; the reason why we are here.

Kippah A small skull cap worn by Jewish men for religious reasons.

L

Life after death The belief that after a person's body dies, a spiritual part of them lives on in another dimension.

Lord's Prayer The prayer Jesus taught his followers. It is the most important prayer for Christians because it contains all the things Jesus said were essential in a prayer.

M

Makkah The holiest city in Islam where prophet Muhammad was born. Muslims face Makkah for daily prayer.

Mass Means a Christian festival. Roman Catholic Christians also use the term for Holy Communion (*see page 124*).

Muhammad The most important prophet in Islam who was responsible for founding the faith as it is today.

N

Near-death experience A term used to describe what some people experience when their heart has stopped beating for a short time and they have been pronounced clinically dead.

Nelson Mandela The first black president of South Africa. Mandela has been an influential leader who campaigned for a peaceful end to discrimination on the basis of colour.

New Testament A section of the Bible which contains the Christian scriptures.

O

Old Testament The largest section of the Bible which contains the history of the Jewish people and prophesies about the coming of Jesus.

P

Pacifist A person who does not believe in fighting and refuses to go to war.

Perpetrator A person who causes harm to a victim.

Pilgrim A person who makes a special journey for religious reasons.

Prophesy Something written which foretells a future event.

Prophet A messenger sent by God to bring God's words to the people.

Q

Qiblah wall A wall in the mosque which faces the direction of the holy city of Makkah. Muslims pray in front of this wall.

Qur'an The Muslim holy book which is in Arabic, the language in which God gave it to Muhammad.

R

Ramadan A holy month in the Islamic calendar.

Rebirth The belief held by Buddhists that after death, a person's life force will reappear in another person, or in more than one person.

Reconciliation Making peace as a result of forgiveness being given and received.

Reincarnation The belief that after death a person will be reborn as another person. This idea is held by Hindus and Sikhs.

Resurrection of Jesus The time when Jesus came to life again after he had been dead for three days.

Rosh Hashanah The Jewish festival of new year which lasts 10 days and requires Jews to repent of their sins and ask for God's forgiveness.

S

Scriptures Holy books.

Sea of Galilee The place in Israel where Jesus did much of his teachings.

Sikhism The youngest of the six major world religions. Sikhism began in India.

Supernatural experience Something that can not be explained by any known scientific theories.

T

Tallit A prayer shawl worn by a Jewish man.

Tefillin Two leather boxes with straps attached which are worn on the head and arm for morning prayer by a Jewish man.

Theist The term for a person who believes there is a God.

V

Vendetta Feud between two people, or two groups, which is endless. It is very destructive because the action of one side is always repaid by a worse action from the opposite side.

W

Waheguru A chant used by Sikhs in their worship. It means 'Wonderful God'.

Well of Zamzam A place on the Muslim pilgrimage of Hajj that commemorates the time God provided water to save the lives of Hajar and her son.

Western Wall, Jerusalem This is the holiest place for Jews because it is the last remaining part of the Temple.

Wudu A ritual wash Muslims perform before prayer to purify themselves before they approach God.

Y

Yad Vashem A pilgrimage site in Jerusalem. Jews go there to remember the six million Jews who were killed by the Nazis in the Second World War. There are many monuments at Yad Vashem, including one to the million and a half children who were murdered.

Index